MATT CHANDLER

The Apostles' Creed

TOGETHER WE BELIEVE

Lifeway Press®

Nashville, Tennessee

Published by Lifeway Press® • © 2017 The Village Church
Reprinted Sept. 2017, Feb. 2018, July 2018, Nov. 2018, Jan. 2022

ISBN 9781430064688 • Item 005791930
Dewey decimal classification: 238
Subject headings: APOSTLES' CREED / GOSPEL / DOCTRINAL THEOLOGY

To order additional copies of this resource, write to Lifeway Resources Customer
Service; One Lifeway Plaza; Nashville, TN 37234-0113; fax 615.251.5933; phone
toll free 800.458.2772; order online at lifeway.com; email orderentry@lifeway.com.

Printed in the United States of America

Student Ministry Publishing • Lifeway Resources
One Lifeway Plaza • Nashville, TN 37234

Contents

Week 1

Week 2

Week 3

Week 4

Week 5

Week 6

Week 7

Week 8

Week 9

Week 10

Week 11

Week 12

I believe in God the Father Almighty,
    Creator of heaven and earth,
And in Jesus Christ, His only Son, our Lord,
Who was conceived by the Holy Spirit;
    born of the virgin Mary;
Suffered under Pontius Pilate;
    was crucified, dead, and buried.
He descended to hell; the third day
    He rose again from the dead;
He ascended to heaven and sits on the
    right hand of the Father Almighty,
From whence He shall come to judge
    the living and the dead.
I believe in the Holy Spirit,
The holy catholic church,
    the communion of saints,
The forgiveness of sins,
The resurrection of the body,
    and the life everlasting. Amen.

Introduction

We live in a culture that is constantly telling students that they can believe whatever they want and live however they want. The only invalid belief in our culture is to believe that someone else is wrong. This sort of thinking is not only found outside the church but also within. In our day and age of so many different beliefs and worldviews, even in the church, it can be difficult to get to the bottom of what is true and essential to the Christian faith.

The Apostles' Creed is rooted in the apostles' teachings and contains essential Christian doctrines and beliefs that summarize the gospel and make up the foundation of our faith. The scriptural truths contained in the creed help us operate from good theology, with the knowledge that our faith is rooted in truth and a rich history that spans past, present and future. The lines of the creed aren't mere words. They are the essence of what we confess and believe as the body of Christ. In an anything goes culture, the Apostles' Creed gives us the foundation we need to know the truth of the gospel so that it might set us free!

Author

MATT CHANDLER serves as the lead pastor of teaching at The Village Church in the Dallas/Fort Worth metroplex. He came to The Village in December 2002 and describes his tenure as a replanting effort to change the theological and philosophical culture of the congregation. The church has witnessed a tremendous response, growing from 160 people to more than 11,000, including campuses in Flower Mound, Dallas, Plano, and Fort Worth.

Alongside his current role as lead pastor, Matt is involved in church-planting efforts both locally and internationally through The Village, as well as in various strategic partnerships. Prior to accepting the pastorate at The Village, Matt had a vibrant itinerant ministry for more than 10 years that gave him the opportunity to speak to thousands of people in America and abroad about the glory of God and the beauty of Jesus.

Matt is the author of *To Live Is Christ to Die is Gain, Mingling of Souls,* and *The Explicit Gospel Bible Study* (Lifeway, 2012). He's also a coauthor of *Creature of the Word* (Lifeway, 2012).

Other than knowing Jesus, Matt's greatest joy is being married to Lauren and being the dad to their three children, Audrey, Reid, and Norah.

How to Use This Study

Apostles' Creed provides a guided process for individuals and small groups to explore 12 core tenants of Christianity. This Bible study book includes 12 weeks of content, each divided into 2 main sections: Video Guide, Group Study, and Personal Study. We've also developed a Leader Guide to help prepare those leading a group through this journey.

GROUP STUDY

START

Regardless of the day of the week your group meets, each week of content begins by watching the video. Each video is 10-15 minutes long and the Watch section is designed to help you engage directly with the content of the video. Encourage the members of your group to follow along as they watch the video and write their answers to its questions. This will prepare them to engage more deeply in the group study.

WATCH

Each group study is designed to last 30-45 minutes. The goal is to dig deeper into the content and implications of the creed and to help students apply its gospel truths to their daily lives. The format is designed to facilitate simple yet meaningful interaction among group members, with God's Word, and with the video teaching.

DISCUSS

This page includes discussion questions that guide the group to respond to the video teaching and to relevant Bible passages. In this section you will challenge students to interact directly with the content of the Creed by looking to the Scriptures that provide the foundation to the truth of the Creed. Students will not only dig into the text but also wrestle with how the truths of the creed should be applied in their daily lives and in their church and student groups.

PERSONAL STUDY

Three personal studies are provided each week to take individuals deeper into Scripture and to supplement the content introduced in the Group Study. With biblical teaching and interactive questions, these pages challenge individuals to grow in their understanding of God's Word and to make practical application to their lives.

LEADER GUIDE

On pages 130–142 at the back of this book you'll find a Leader Guide that will help you prepare each week. Use this guide to gain a broad understanding of the content for each week and for suggestions of ways to engage members at different levels of life-changing discussion.

PREPARE

This section outlines everything you need to do to be ready to lead your group through each session, including tips for being spiritually prepared as well as anything you will need to bring.

ENGAGE

This section includes an optional opening activity, illustration, or discussion to introduce each session's theme.

WATCH

Play the video and encourage students to follow along in the video guide. Use the discussion questions as you talk through the video with your students. Videos are available to rent or purchase at lifeway.com/apostlescreed.

BRING IT HOME

This section equips leaders with application challenges, questions, or activities to close out their group time.

Each leader guide concludes with a prayer directive that helps leaders guide their students in praying through each section of the Apostles' Creed.

Apostles' Creed Grid

Throughout this study we'll examine and apply the doctrines outlined in the Apostles' Creed by using a four-part grid as a filter to draw out key truths. The first session will introduce the grid, and the following sessions (weeks 2–12) will explore a specific phrase in the creed by examining it through each of the four areas of focus and application.

SYMMETRY: *The creed helps us develop a deeper, more knowledgeable faith—to know what we believe and why.*

As Christians, it's easy to stick with what we already know. Either we don't grow and remain immature with a minimal, two-dimensional faith, or even if we're growing, we become out of balance instead of developing a deep, well-rounded faith. The creed helps us intentionally cover the key truths of the Bible. Think of it like an exercise routine. Just as you don't need to work the same muscle group every day, neglecting the others, you need to broaden your understanding of the full scope of biblical truth. Believing Jesus is your Savior is vital, but it's also necessary to recognize that He's called you into a relationship with the church. A Christian who settles for believing in Jesus as his personal Savior but never develops a love for the church is out of balance and ultimately unhealthy. We desire balance to be well rounded in our doctrinal understanding as mature disciples.

CLARITY: *The creed helps us with clarity, making clear who God is.*

While symmetry applies to our overall knowledge of core biblical doctrines, clarity is a more specific focus on what we believe about God and the world. By and large, American evangelicals seem to be terribly confused about who God is, what He's up to, what He's like, and what He's about. Surveys reveal shocking misconceptions, many of which are similar to the false doctrines that the Apostles' Creed was intended to correct. For example, is Jesus both fully God and fully man? Did Jesus literally die? Did He have a physical body when He rose from the dead? The Christian life isn't about our preferences or opinions or the latest cultural trends; it's about God. What you believe about God is the most important thing in your life; it shapes all your attitudes and actions.

COMMUNITY: *The creed informs our community, whom we belong to, and whom we're with.*

As Christians who believe the doctrines summarized in the Apostles' Creed, we're part of a people who have been around for thousands of years. We're part of a people who go back to the beginning of humankind, when God called the first people to Himself. Throughout history God's people, His elect, those He has called to Himself, have thrived and worshiped the one true God. We're part of that tradition. We're a global people. People all over the earth will gather this weekend because they share the beliefs expressed in the creed. They'll rejoice in it, they'll be shaped by it, and many of them will even recite the creed together. We have been woven into something much bigger than us. The fabric created by God makes us stronger than any of us can ever be on our own. It's diverse, it's beautiful, and it's global.

As Christianity in the United States, having enjoyed great favor the past 150 years, now starts to fall out of favor, any effort to define ourselves by secondary beliefs must also fade away. The creed shows us what's of most importance in the Christian faith. We're a creedal people, united by truth that trumps any other differences in our culture and sets us apart as a distinct community of faith.

COUNSEL: *The creed informs the way we counsel ourselves and others.*

Counsel is essentially the point of application. How do symmetry, clarity, and community lead to a change in your perspective? How do these things lead you to think and act differently? What do you tell yourself or others as a result of believing the doctrines in the creed? For example, if you believe Christ will return to judge the living and dead, that will affect the way you think about sin and the way you warn and encourage others in regard to personal holiness. Think of the ammunition that belief provides against sin. When you grow in your understanding of the person of God, the work of Christ, and the power of the Holy Spirit, you'll think differently.

The four parts of this grid work together to form a cohesive framework to help us grow within the long tradition of orthodox Christian beliefs. Symmetry in our understanding of the Bible leads to more clarity about who God is. The better we understand God and the big picture of the Bible, the better we can counsel ourselves and one another in the community of faith. As we counsel one another in community, we grow in symmetry and clarity. The result should be an ever-deepening maturity and a closer walk of obedience with our Lord Jesus Christ.

Week One

I believe in God the Father Almighty,
    Creator of heaven and earth,
And in Jesus Christ, His only Son, our Lord,
Who was conceived by the Holy Spirit;
    born of the virgin Mary;
Suffered under Pontius Pilate;
    was crucified, dead, and buried.
He descended to hell; the third day
    He rose again from the dead;
He ascended to heaven and sits on the
    right hand of the Father Almighty,
From whence He shall come to judge
    the living and the dead.
I believe in the Holy Spirit,
The holy catholic church,
    the communion of saints,
The forgiveness of sins,
The resurrection of the body,
    and the life everlasting. Amen.

Group Study

START

I BELIEVE IN

Welcome to session 1 of The Apostles' Creed.

Let's begin by taking a few minutes to get to know one another.

Introduce yourself by sharing your name and favorite sport or activity.

Have you ever been to a concert of a popular band or big sporting event? What was the atmosphere like?

Few things today bring people together today more than big concerts and sporting events. Stadiums are, in many ways, the temples of worship of our culture. The excitement and fervor with which people gather together and cheer at such events creates a powerful sense of confidence, pride, and identity. We all desire to belong to something greater than ourselves. Such concerts and games are some of the few places left in our individualistic and divided culture where diverse people unite around a common purpose.

The Apostles' Creed is a simple yet profound document that Christians have relied upon for over 1,600 years to root themselves in common belief and purpose. We live in a culture that does not have a firm foundation—one that is constantly telling us that we can believe whatever we want and live however we want. As we study the Apostles Creed, we will seek to recover the core truths that have provided a firm foundation and directed the lives of Christians for centuries.

Read the following Scripture
before watching the video for session 1:

Faith is the assurance of things hoped for, the conviction of things not seen. For by it the people of old received their commendation.
HEBREWS 11:1-2

WATCH

*Use this viewer guide to follow along and
take notes as you watch video session 1.*

The Apostles' Creed will help us with:
1. Symmetry—a robust understanding of the Bible
2. Clarity—who God is
3. Community—whom we belong to and whom we're with
4. Counsel—to ourselves and to others

A creed is a document that lays out the essential beliefs of a religion. Creeds do not hold any authority in and of themselves, but rather, they point outside themselves to the ultimate authority of the Word of God.

The Apostles' Creed has been used—
- to correct false teaching;
- as a tool in the spiritual formation of God's people.

Believing is different than knowing. Believing leads to action, and knowing may or may not.

Belief is birthed in the heart.

As we look at the Apostles' Creed, we will see that the message of Christianity is not "do this or that," but rather about what our God has done. That does not mean that the Creed does not demand anything of us—the Creed demands everything from us—it asks us to believe.

The Apostles' Creed shows us what is primary.

The message of the Christian faith isn't that we have done anything, but rather that we have believed that Someone else has. This is the primary difference between the gospel and every other religion.

We aren't chained to rote religious activity, but we have a Savior who has accomplished all that we desire for us.

**Videos sessions are available at
lifeway.com/apostlescreed.**

DISCUSS

Discuss this week's video using the following questions.

From now on we'll begin each session by reciting the Apostles' Creed together as a group. Let's pause now to read it aloud. You can find it on page 10.

Why do you think Christians have recited the words of this creed for centuries together in churches?

What is significant about the first word of the Apostles' Creed?

Why is it important for Christians to articulate and agree on what we believe?

Why did Matt distinguish between the authority of Scripture and of a creed? How is the authority of Scripture greater?

READ ROMANS 10:9-10.

How do belief and action relate to salvation? What distinction did Matt make between knowing and believing?

In what specific ways do our historical Christian beliefs, as outlined in the Apostles' Creed, rebel against our present-day culture?

How does a Christian experience freedom in believing the gospel?

Because the Apostles' Creed is a faithful and right summary of Christian doctrine as revealed in the Bible, notice that no article of the creed can be removed without detracting from the gospel. Every point is essential.

What's your primary takeaway in response to Matt's teaching on belief?

Make time this week to complete the following personal studies before the next group session.

Personal Study

DAY 1

The Apostles' Creed begins with the words "I believe in." When you recite the creed in your group each week, you're declaring to the world that you believe the Christian story is both good and true. God the Father is reconciling the world to Himself in the Person and work of Jesus Christ, through the power of the Holy Spirit.

The creed is more than just a statement of individual belief. It articulates what has been and should be most important to every member of Christ's church. You're "surrounded by so great a cloud of witnesses" (Heb. 12:1) and publicly identifying with the church—a group of people who believe in the triune God.

In the early church, uttering the word *credo* ("I believe") meant identifying in the closest possible way with Christ. Often a new believer recited the Apostles' Creed during his baptism and was then welcomed into the membership of the church. When someone said the creed, he was identifying himself as a citizen of a different kingdom—the kingdom of God. This world in its present state is not our home—we belong to a greater king and a greater kingdom and this reality changes everything for us. The creed is more than just a list of important information—its filled with truth that gives us ultimate hope and shapes our ultimate purpose in life.

READ HEBREWS 11:1-2.

The beauty and tension of these verses come from the fact that based on what has happened in the past, Christians have assurance and conviction in placing their hope and belief in something they've never seen.

Though we believe in the existence of God since before time began and in His work that began human history with the creation of the world, a man named Abram was the first in a long tradition of people who put their belief in God.

READ GENESIS 12:1-4.

We learn more about Abram, later called Abraham, throughout the pages of Scripture in a stunning account of a genuine belief in action. His story is central in the historical record of faith recorded in Hebrews 11.

Why do you think details about Abram's age, family, and land were included in Genesis 12:1-4? What do they reveal about belief?

What experiences have challenged you to consider how seriously you believe something about God and/or His Word? How might we be sure that we genuinely believe?

Abram's belief in God affected his own life, the lives of his family members, and the lives of people around him. The same is true today. Your beliefs have been shaped by other people; your faith is a testimony that affects the people around you as well.

Who is someone you admire for their faith. How does their faith stand out? What have you learned from their example?

We are made for community, and that's why the creed is meant to be confessed together with other believers. However, even when the creed is recited in unison by a local congregation, the first word of each statement of the creed is *I*. Popular culture asserts that all people should have the opportunity, even the right, to define themselves. The Apostles' Creed reminds us that the truth isn't up for redefinition. The creed reminds us that Christ defines who we are as individuals and calls us to live in community, helping one another live out our identity in Him.

Prayer

Grant me faith, Father in heaven. Give me a faith that's focused on Your work, the work of Your Son, and the work of the Holy Spirit throughout the history of the world. Even when I struggle to believe, strengthen me by Your grace. Help me walk by faith, not by sight, and grow my love for You as I learn more about Your mighty deeds. Help me stay true to the faith that was handed down to me, help me see myself as you see me—redeemed to live for your kingdom. Amen.

DAY 2

Whether or not people go to church and whether or not they know what the verse says, it's hard to go through life without seeing a reference to John 3:16.

Use this space to write John 3:16 from memory. If you don't have the verse memorized, look it up in your Bible and copy it here.

How would you explain the importance of belief, according to John 3:16?

Describe the moment when you first believed in Jesus. If you haven't had a moment like this in your life, record the name of your group leader and/or a trusted Christian friend whom you'll commit to ask questions about personal belief in Jesus.

This popular verse is part of a conversation Jesus had with a Jewish leader named Nicodemus (see John 3:1-21). Jesus' words boldly declared what it means to believe in God. In that culture the many of the Jewish people had grown to believe that their relationship and right standing before God were based on two things: observing Jewish religious traditions and being born into Jewish families. However, Jesus said anyone could have a relationship with God—if they truly believed in His Son for salvation.

A similar trap of mistaken belief in what makes people right with God exists today. If someone grew up in a Christian home or is a morally good person, it's easy to believe he or she is a Christian. The Bible is crystal clear, though, about the fact that merely believing correct things about God won't get anybody into heaven.

THIS POINT CAN'T BE OVERSTATED:
YOUR GOOD WORKS WON'T SAVE YOU.

In which area(s) do you find yourself inclined to measure your relationship with God? By which criteria do you evaluate other people?

- **Being obedient to teachers and parents**
- **Following the rules**
- **Going to church**
- **Studying the Bible**
- **Volunteering to serve**
- **Making good grades**
- **Being recognized as a leader**

What's the danger of basing the certainty of your salvation on external behaviors like those above?

Pisteuō, the Greek word translated as *believes* in John 3:16, has a richer meaning than the simple understanding of facts. To believe in something means to commit and to give your trust. When you truly believe something, you act on it. Belief isn't just a matter of head knowledge. It's a matter of the heart's devotion.

It's easy for John 3:16 to become so familiar that the gravity of the situation is lost. Don't let words like *love, life,* and *saved* distract you from *perish* and *condemned.* You need to wrestle with each of those realities until you come to grips with what's at stake here. Belief that is nothing more than an adherence to rules or knowledge of religious facts is not true belief. True belief is a life-changing commitment and trust—it is a matter of eternal life or death.

Prayer

Spend time reflecting on the fact that your relationship with God isn't based on who you are, where you were born, or what you know. Thank Him that you can live eternally as part of His family by truly believing in His only Son, Jesus. Commit yourself to trust Christ wholeheartedly.

Unlike Matthew and Luke, John didn't begin his Gospel account by providing a detailed record of Jesus' birth. Instead, the Gospel of John begins with a beautiful description of the divine personhood and redemptive purpose of Jesus' incarnation.

READ JOHN 1:11-13.

What's the result of belief in Christ, according to these verses?

From the very beginning of the book, John told his readers that Jesus came so that their lives could be changed forever by believing in Him. The opening words revealed that through faith in Jesus, anyone could become a child of God. However, the people who should have recognized and believed in Jesus—the Jews—didn't receive Him.

The account of Nicodemus in John 3 illustrates the lack of understanding among God's people. He was a religious expert who couldn't wrap his mind around the truth of salvation by faith in the Son of God. This Jewish leader couldn't understand how "whoever believes in" Jesus (v. 16) could be born again into God's eternal family.

As John concluded his book, he brought an unmistakable conclusion to everything he had written about what it means to believe in Jesus.

READ JOHN 20:24-31.

Notice that Jesus didn't leave Thomas in a state of confusion and doubt. Jesus met this disciple in the midst of his struggle to believe. Thomas had been a devoted follower of Jesus. He had committed to literally follow Jesus every day for almost three years. He had put his trust in Jesus. But after the crucifixion, Thomas didn't know what was true.

Try to imagine yourself in his position. It would have been difficult to trust your own judgment and hopes after such an traumatic experience. The person you respected and loved the most died! Of course, you would have wanted to believe Jesus had been raised from the dead, but no one in history has ever risen from the dead.

What have you struggled to believe about the Christian faith?

In what ways is it comforting to read that even one of Jesus' disciples struggled with whether he could believe what he was being told about Jesus?

What objections do people have about Christianity?

Whom do you know who has doubts about the Christian faith?

How might we help our friends and family work through their doubts and objections?

How can you help share the truth about your Lord and your God, the resurrected Jesus?

The Gospel of John comes full circle in the final words of the book. John clearly restated in unmistakable terms his desire for the church. As a believer, you are a part of this legacy.

Prayer

Thank God that in His grace He has come to you, speaking your name, so that you can believe in His Son, Jesus Christ. Take time to worship Him now as your personal Lord and Savior.

Week Two

I believe in God the Father Almighty,
    Creator of heaven and earth,
And in Jesus Christ, His only Son, our Lord,
Who was conceived by the Holy Spirit;
    born of the virgin Mary;
Suffered under Pontius Pilate;
    was crucified, dead, and buried.
He descended to hell; the third day
    He rose again from the dead;
He ascended to heaven and sits on the
    right hand of the Father Almighty,
From whence He shall come to judge
    the living and the dead.
I believe in the Holy Spirit,
The holy catholic church,
    the communion of saints,
The forgiveness of sins,
The resurrection of the body,
    and the life everlasting. Amen.

Group Study

START

GOD THE FATHER ALMIGHTY, CREATOR OF HEAVEN AND EARTH

Welcome to session 2 of The Apostles' Creed.

Let's begin by taking a few minutes to review this past week's study.

Why are creeds and statements of faith important? How are they helpful? What benefit is there in knowing the Apostles' Creed? In reciting it together with other believers?

Day 2 of the personal study included a checklist of things other than faith with which we may be tempted to measure our Christian identities and relationships with God. Which did you select and why?

Last week we established the importance of belief. From this point on we'll focus on specific doctrines that make up the core of our Christian faith. This week we begin our study where the Bible begins: "God the Father Almighty, Creator of heaven and earth."

Read the Apostles' Creed aloud as a group
before watching the video for session 2.

WATCH

*Use this viewer guide to follow along and
take notes as you watch video session 2.*

1. SYMMETRY

The Bible is vocal and loud about God's delight in you, His pleasure in you,
and His desire for a personal relationship with you.

Our God is an infinitely powerful and yet intensely personal Father.

We all have a tendency to think of Him as one or the other. Both are vital to our
faith—we serve a God who is infinitely powerful and yet He makes Himself near
to us.

The gospel not only reconciles us to the Father, but then begins to reconcile us to
one another.

2. CLARITY

To be a God of love is to have wrath.

God proves His love by refusing to turn a blind eye to our selfish and destructive
actions and attitudes.

If God loves you, He will expose your secret sin.

3. COMMUNITY

God has not only called us to Himself but also to each other.

We walk together as the communion of saints brought together by our Father.

4. COUNSEL

If God the Father almighty is infinitely powerful and intensely personal,
that should shape how we counsel ourselves and others.

Do you believe that God is good? Do you believe that God is for you and not
against you regardless of your life circumstances? If you believe these two things
you can join with the refrain of Christians across 2,000 years of history who have
said, "I believe in God the Father almighty creator of heaven and earth."

DISCUSS

Discuss this week's video using the following questions.

We all have to wrestle with the question of whether we believe God is good. Why is that question foundational?

When have you struggled to believe God is good? When have you wanted something and didn't understand why God wasn't saying yes?

What is the difference between deism and Christianity?

How does it affect your view of God to know that He delights in you? How does it affect your view of yourself?

Why do love and wrath necessarily go together in God's character? Why would a loving God expose secret sin?

How should the fact that God is infinitely powerful and intensely personal shape our daily lives? Our relationships?

Which of the two attributes do you tend to think of most when you think about God: powerful or personal? Why do you relate to Him in that way? Why is it vital to relate to God as both/and, not either/or?

READ MATTHEW 6:9-13.

How does each phrase in the Lord's Prayer reveal God's character as both personal and powerful?

What's your primary takeaway in response to the teaching on "God the Father Almighty, Creator of heaven and earth"?

Remember to complete the following personal studies before the next group session.

Personal Study

Have you ever been in darkness so complete that you literally couldn't see your hand in front of your face? No amount of time can allow your eyes to adjust when you're in total darkness. Now imagine a full moon on a dark night. It allows you to see the world around you in a way that would otherwise be impossible. Now imagine being in that same spot in the middle of a sunny day. You have a clear, more complete picture.

The Apostles' Creed is like the moon. It's not the source of light. As the moon reflects the light of the sun, the creed merely reflects the truth of Scripture. God's Word is the sun—our source of truth. Remember that you aren't studying the creed. It's a summary of what we believe. You're studying the Bible. It's the totality of what we believe. The creed should point you to the truth revealed in God's Word.

The creed starts where the Bible starts: with God.

READ GENESIS 1:1.

The Bible begins with one of the most stunning, reality-shaping phrases possible.

What's the first thing we learn about God from this verse? Why is this an important starting point for the entire Bible?

God created from nothing. He didn't simply fashion preexisting creation into new shapes and forms; He brought creation into being by His word (see Gen. 1; Heb. 11:3). By the incomparable power of His will, God spoke everything into existence. He's Almighty.

READ PSALM 8.

Where do you see God's power and creativity on display in the world today? What's impresses you most about God's creation?

How should believing that God created you as uniquely valuable shape the way you see yourself? How should this reality shape the way you think about your purpose in life?

As the Apostles' Creed states, God the Father Almighty is the "Creator of heaven and earth." Referring to Christ, theologian Abraham Kuyper said, "There is not a square inch in the whole domain of our human existence over which Christ, who is Sovereign over *all,* does not cry: 'Mine!'"[1] These words beautifully capture the fact that every bit of every created thing rightly belongs to God.

Why is it important to believe in the fact that God is all-powerful and has authority over all things?

What areas of your life are you most tempted to deny as being under God's supreme authority? Why?

What actions will you take to acknowledge that everything belongs to God?

Prayer

Father, by Your mighty word, You've brought all things into existence.
I can rightly call You my Maker and Creator. Everything belongs to You,
my Father. Continually give me eyes to see Your beauty and ears to
hear Your marvelous truth. Thank You that not only are You my Creator,
but You're also my Father. Draw me ever closer into fellowship with
You, through the work of Your Son and by Your Holy Spirit. Amen.

1. Abraham Kuyper, as quoted in *Abraham Kuyper: A Centennial Reader,*
   ed. James D. Bratt (Grand Rapids, MI: Eerdmans, 1998), 461.

DAY 2

Although God is the Almighty, holy Creator of all things, He isn't a generic deity. The God of the Bible has given Himself to us as the Trinity. We believe God has eternally existed as one essence and three distinct Persons: God the Father, God the Son, and God the Holy Spirit. Each Person is fully God, yet at the same time, there's only one God. Specifically, this part of the Creed addresses the first Person of the Godhead—God the Father.

The first line of the Apostles' Creed confesses that we believe in God the Father. This line clearly indicates that we don't believe in a God who's far off and distant, but a God who's infinitely powerful yet intensely personal.

List as many characteristics as you can that describe a good father.

READ EPHESIANS 1:3-14.

In what ways does God act like a father to us, His children? List the different descriptions of God in this passage and identify what He has done for His children.

Why is it important to believe that God had a plan for your life since the beginning of time?

How should it affect the way you live today, as you face different decisions, circumstances, and relationships, to know that God has a plan for the future?

Consider the meaning of an inheritance from your parents. How does this concept apply to our relationship with God? What's the inheritance for people who've been adopted by God to be His children?

Have you wrestled with any obstacles to trusting that the Father's care for you is best? If so, list them here.

How has God the Father shown faithfulness and love to you and your family?

With whom can you share what you've experienced to be true about a relationship with God through faith in Christ?

Prayer

Thank God for His generous, sacrificial love for you, expressed in the giving of His Son, Jesus, and of His Holy Spirit. Confess any areas of your life in which you aren't trusting His will and glorifying His name as your good Father. Ask God for wisdom to recognize opportunities to share the good news of salvation from sin, adoption through faith in Christ, and the hope of eternal life as a coheir in the family of God.

Because every believer enjoys a personal relationship with God, the creed reminds us that we're also in fellowship with the millions of Christians around the world and from every age who believe these truths about God found in the creed.

Our belief in God is more than a theological point of agreement about correct doctrine. A right understanding of God is foundational to right living. It has practical implications for our relationships with God and one another. Let's review this week's points of symmetry, clarity, community, and counsel that arise from belief in God.

1. SYMMETRY

First, as our Creator, God knows what's best for us. He made us. A creator of something knows how it works best, right? God created everything. He created the heavens and the earth and everything in them—including you. Everything has a purpose. The design is intentional, detailed, and beautiful. Throughout the story of creation, the common refrain in Genesis 1 is "It was good." The Bible is vocal and loud about God's delight in you, His pleasure in you, and His desire to be with you. In other words, He loves you.

> **How does it affect the way you relate to God when you believe that He created you and wants what's best for you?**

2. CLARITY

Because a father is wiser than his children, he wants what's best for them, even if they don't understand or like it at the moment. As part of God's family through belief in His only Son (see John 3:16), we have to take seriously the consequences of rebellion.

Sin is rebellion against the good design of our Creator and the loving desire of our Father. We need to realize that sin destroys us and our relationship with God. Because God knows and wants what's best for us, He hates sin. Because He loves us, He pours out wrath on that which destroys us and our relationships with Him and one another.

READ HEBREWS 12:5-11.

> **How does viewing God as Father affect the way you think about sin? The way you view correction and discipline?**

3. COMMUNITY

READ GALATIANS 3:26-28 AND 1 JOHN 3.

How should belief in God as a good Creator and a loving Father change
the way you view and treat other people? Whom have you not been
treating as a brother or a sister, created and loved by God?

4. COUNSEL

By the authority of God's word at creation, we've been made His children. What
He says to be true is true. A right belief in God also gives each person in the family
of God the responsibility of reminding one another of the seriousness of sin. If
our Father's love includes wrath toward sin, then we should love members of His
family enough to address sin and to welcome correction from others when they
confront our sin.

Who will speak truth into your life as a brother or a sister through faith
in Christ? Whom do you need to remind of the goodness of God or of
the seriousness of sin?

Prayer

Take a few minutes to let the profound reality of 1 John 3:1 sink into your heart.
In this one simple statement you can see God as both a powerful Creator
and a loving Father. Pray that this truth will reorient your life, giving you a
confidence in and conviction of the awesome privilege of being a child of God.

Week Three

I believe in God the Father Almighty,
   Creator of heaven and earth,
And in Jesus Christ, His only Son, our Lord,
Who was conceived by the Holy Spirit;
   born of the virgin Mary;
Suffered under Pontius Pilate;
   was crucified, dead, and buried.
He descended to hell; the third day
   He rose again from the dead;
He ascended to heaven and sits on the
   right hand of the Father Almighty,
From whence He shall come to judge
   the living and the dead.
I believe in the Holy Spirit,
The holy catholic church,
   the communion of saints,
The forgiveness of sins,
The resurrection of the body,
   and the life everlasting. Amen.

𝔊𝔯𝔬𝔲𝔭 𝔖𝔱𝔲𝔡𝔶

START

AND IN JESUS CHRIST, HIS ONLY SON, OUR LORD

Welcome to session 3 of The Apostles' Creed.

Let's begin by taking a few minutes to review this past week's study.

Why is it important that we believe that God is all powerful and all good? That He is infinitely greater than us and yet desires to draw near to us?

Day 3 of each week from now on calls for interaction with the grid Matt introduced for understanding and applying the core doctrines summarized in the Apostles' Creed. Which of the four areas were most applicable this week and why? (Refer to pp. 28–29 if needed.)

1. **Symmetry: a balanced, robust understanding of the Bible**
2. **Clarity: a picture of who God truly is, not who we want Him to be**
3. **Community: an understanding of how to relate to one another as Christians**
4. **Counsel: an ability to speak biblical truth to ourselves and to others**

While not as explicit as the Nicene Creed, with its clear articulation of the divine relationship within the Trinity, the Apostles' Creed is unmistakably trinitarian. This week we move from "God the Father" to the second Person of the Trinity: "Jesus Christ, His only Son, our Lord."

Read the Apostles' Creed aloud as a group before watching the video for session 3.

WATCH

*Use this viewer guide to follow along and
take notes as you watch video session 3.*

This section of the Creed assigns three titles to Jesus: "the Christ," the "Son of God," and "Lord." Each reveals something about who Jesus is and what He came to do.

Jesus is the King of everything.

JESUS IS UNIQUE IN HIS SONSHIP

1. He is co-eternal with God the Father.

2. He walks in a distinct authority.

3. He is a part of the Godhead.

When Jesus is called Lord, He is called the Savior of the world.

1. SYMMETRY
Jesus is King over all things—He is absolute in power.

2. CLARITY
We can do nothing to stop Jesus.

3. COMMUNITY
If we could understand how weak and impossible our situation is we would grow in reverence for the kingship of Jesus Christ. And yet, in His kingly domain which extends over everything, He uses His authority to save, to rescue, and to woo us. He is a tender King, not a tyrant.

4. COUNSEL
As Almighty Lord and merciful Savior, Jesus is worthy. He is worthy of all that we are and all that we have.

DISCUSS

Discuss this week's video using the following questions.

What do other students at your school, on your team, or in your neighborhood say about Jesus? How do they view Him?

READ MATTHEW 16:13-16.

How does what people say about Jesus compare with who He truly is? How can we know what Jesus is actually like?

Why is it important to recognize and confess Jesus as Christ (Savior), God's only Son, and Lord (King)?

Why is it common in our culture to claim Jesus as Savior without submitting to Him as King?

If Jesus is who He says He is, we cannot be indifferent to that claim. Why can't we remain indifferent to Jesus? What are the consequences for doing so?

Sin is rebellion against God. What has God done for rebellious sinners like us? What makes the gospel such good news? How does it unite us as Christians?

How does living according to God's design bring joy? What is one way you will submit to Christ as your Lord this week?

What's your biggest takeaway in response to the teaching on "And in Jesus Christ, His only Son, our Lord"?

Don't forget to complete the following personal studies before the next group session.

Personal Study

DAY 1

If you attended a function at which Queen Elizabeth was present, she wouldn't be introduced to you as Liz Windsor. She would be presented as "Her Majesty Elizabeth II, by the grace of God of the United Kingdom of Great Britain and Northern Ireland and of her other realms and territories queen, head of the commonwealth, defender of the faith." Her title is more than just a name, each part explains her identity. The same can be said of this week's portion of the Apostles' Creed. It presents God's Son to us in terms that communicate who He is and the authority He commands.

When God made the birth of Jesus known to His earthly father, Joseph, two names were given: Jesus and Immanuel (see Matt. 1:18-25). The Gospel of Matthew explains that Immanuel means "God with us" (v. 23). The account reveals that Jesus is the incarnate God. The name Jesus, a common name at the time, means "The Lord saves." When we see the name Jesus, we're reminded of our Lord as both the Son of God and the historical man who bore that name. Jesus' earthly name points us to the truth of His full humanity.

READ ROMANS 1:1-4.

What evidence do these verses present for Jesus' humanity and divinity?

True belief in Jesus is at the heart of a relationship with God. The most popular verse in the Bible summarizes the gospel of Jesus, including His identity:

> *God so loved the world that He gave His only begotten Son, that whoever believes in Him should not perish but have everlasting life.*
> **JOHN 3:16, NKJV**

Begotten, to modern ears, sounds like a synonym for *created.* However, the Greek word from which it's translated is *monogeneses,* does not express that Jesus was created, but that He's uniquely God the Son. Jesus is equal in substance and co-eternal with the Father. Jesus has always been God but there was a moment in time when God the Son was "begotten"—He took on flesh, and dwelt with us. Even before the incarnation, the second Person of the Trinity was always—and is eternally—the Son of the Father (see Col. 1:15-20).

READ HEBREWS 1.

Last week you studied some key characteristics of God. How did the writer of Hebrews describe Jesus? What does this tell you about Him?

READ HEBREWS 2:17-18.

Why is it essential to salvation that Jesus is both fully God and fully man?

READ HEBREWS 4:14-16.

What does this passage say we gain in Jesus' humanity?

The writer of Hebrews used the word *propitiation* to describe the purpose of Jesus' life and death as God and man (see 2:17). Our sin deserves the wrath of God, as we studied last week. In His love for us, God poured out His wrath on His Son for our sin, but also provided grace and mercy through Jesus.

The gospel—the good news—is that Jesus took your place, accepting the punishment for your sin and making peace between you and God (see 2 Cor. 5:21). But Jesus does more than pay for your sin. He helps you live each day in the freedom and joy of knowing that your sin has been forgiven and you have been adopted into God's eternal family. No matter what you're going through, Immanuel is with you.

Prayer

Heavenly Father, help me always remember the beautiful truth that Jesus Christ is fully God and fully man. Thank You that He's both my perfect substitute and my perfect Savior. Help me acknowledge His lordship through a greater obedience to Your commands. In the name of Jesus Christ, my Lord, amen.

While it's difficult, if not impossible, to fully wrap our human minds around the reality that Jesus is 100 percent God and 100 percent man, the glorious mystery of God's love for us is clearly revealed in Christ. As the second Person of the Trinity, the Son has made a way for us to become children of God.

READ COLOSSIANS 1:15-20.

What do these verses tell you about Jesus? About His authority? Make a list.

READ MATTHEW 16:13-17.

How would you answer if Jesus asked you the same question He asked Peter, "Who do you say that I am?" (v. 15)? Journal your response.

Peter recognized that there was more to Jesus than people saw. The word *Christ* means "Anointed One" or "Chosen One." It has the same meaning as the Greek word for *Messiah,* the Savior who was predicted throughout the Old Testament. God opened Peter's eyes to this reality. Peter's affirmation was more than factual. It was personal. It was relational.

Nobody can believe for you. It's not enough to know what other people believe about Jesus. The conversation with Peter points out that a lot of people can believe good things about Jesus but can still be wrong about who He truly is.

What opinions, good or bad, have you heard about Jesus? What is lacking in these opinions?

The Bible includes another conversation between Jesus and His disciples about His identity and relationship with God. Once again, Jesus used language relating to a family.

READ JOHN 14:1-6.

Notice that Jesus said, "I am *the* way, and *the* truth, and *the* life" and was then unmistakably clear: *"No one* comes to the Father except through me" (v. 6, emphasis added). The Apostles' Creed is also exclusive and definitive in its wording: *His only* Son.

Jesus may be popular and well respected, but belief in Jesus as the only way to truly know God and to live eternally in heaven is as divisive now as it was when Jesus spoke these words.

If you believe in Jesus as the only Son of God, the only way to know the truth about God, and the only way to eternal life in heaven, then what other religious or philosophical beliefs can't be true?

READ JOHN 14:15.

Faith in Jesus is more than agreeing that He's fully God and fully man. Belief in Jesus is even more than agreeing that He's the only way to know God and to live with Him forever. Saving faith is belief that leads to action.

Think about the different things going on in your life. What do you need to do to obey Jesus in each area of your life?

Prayer

Spend time declaring the truth about Jesus, praising Him for who He is and what He's done for you. Thank God for revealing to you the truth about His only Son.

True Christian belief is more than an opinion about Jesus. It's surrender to His lordship as Savior and King. He's the promised Messiah, the only One who can save us. Therefore, Jesus is worthy of all that we are and all that we have.

Early Christians who professed Jesus as Lord were doing more than claiming to know some things about Jesus; they were declaring allegiance Him as King. The Roman law required everyone to acknowledge Caesar as Lord. Christians who proclaimed that Jesus was Lord were singled out as disloyal to Rome and the prevailing culture. Their disobedience brought condemnation and persecution. Furthermore, the Jewish culture rejected belief in Jesus as the Christ and only Son of God. To believe otherwise was to be rejected by the religious community. Professing the lordship of Christ is central to the gospel in every age because in doing so, Christians declare that Jesus is the true King and Lord of all.

The statement "I believe in . . . Jesus Christ, His only Son, our Lord" brings symmetry, clarity, community, and counsel to the Christian life and witness.

1. SYMMETRY

Time for a gut check. Legitimate, life-or-death persecution has been a part of Christianity since Jesus was crucified. Millions of Christians live with the reality of persecution right now. Though it may be easy to say you're committed to your faith in Jesus, consider your life. Are you trying to claim Jesus as your Savior without submitting to Him as Lord and King? Jesus Himself will not allow us to do this. It's a lie of our self-centered culture to believe we can have the benefits of salvation without the cost of following Jesus.

2. CLARITY

If Jesus is who He says He is, you can't be indifferent to that claim. Is He the way, the truth, and the life or not (see John 14:6)? Is He the only Son, fully God and fully man, or not? Is He Savior and Lord, or not? Like the disciples, you must decide what you believe about Jesus. To be clear, deciding what you believe doesn't mean deciding whether it's true. Truth is truth. You're responsible for what you'll do now that you've heard the truth about Jesus.

How well do your actions line up with what you say you believe about Jesus? Mark a point on the scale that represents your answer.

1	2	3	4	5	6	7	8	9	10
Not at all									Completely

READ MATTHEW 7:21-23.

These are some of the most sobering words in Scripture. We can't take faith and obedience lightly. They're inseparable parts of the Christian life. For Christ to be Savior, He must also be Lord. There's no middle ground. Jesus said we're either in or we're out. If we merely pay lip service and don't submit to Him as King, then we're not a part of His kingdom.

3. COMMUNITY

When you declare, "Jesus is Lord," you join the voices of every believer from the past two thousand years and around the world today. You join your brothers and sisters in Christ. The Apostles' Creed is specific when it says Jesus Christ is "our Lord," not just "the Lord." A confession of personal faith is a commitment to the community of faith.

4. COUNSEL

Jesus said to believe in Him and promised He will return when our eternal home is ready (see John 14:1-6). He's coming back. When He does, He's coming for those in true relationship with Him. We've been given the truth. Live each day for the sake of Jesus Christ, the only Son of God, our Lord.

READ 2 CORINTHIANS 5:16-21.

Prayer

Ask God to give you a desperate burden for reconciliation. In prayer, repent of your sin, submitting to Christ as Lord. Also pray that God will equally burden you with a sense of urgency for others to be reconciled to Him through saving faith in Jesus.

Week Four

I believe in God the Father Almighty,
    Creator of heaven and earth,
And in Jesus Christ, His only Son, our Lord,
Who was conceived by the Holy Spirit;
    born of the virgin Mary;
Suffered under Pontius Pilate;
    was crucified, dead, and buried.
He descended to hell; the third day
    He rose again from the dead;
He ascended to heaven and sits on the
    right hand of the Father Almighty,
From whence He shall come to judge
    the living and the dead.
I believe in the Holy Spirit,
The holy catholic church,
    the communion of saints,
The forgiveness of sins,
The resurrection of the body,
    and the life everlasting. Amen.

𝔊𝔯𝔬𝔲𝔭 𝔖𝔱𝔲𝔡𝔶

START

WHO WAS CONCEIVED BY THE HOLY SPIRIT; BORN OF THE VIRGIN MARY

Welcome to session 4 of The Apostles' Creed.

Let's begin by taking a few minutes to review this past week.

> **Can Jesus be your Savior but not your Lord? Why must we submit to Jesus as Lord?**

> **Day 3 focused on the grid for understanding and applying each of the core doctrines summarized in the Apostles' Creed. Which of the four areas were most applicable this week and why? (Refer to pp. 38–39 if needed.)**

> 1. **Symmetry: a balanced, robust understanding of the Bible**
> 2. **Clarity: a picture of who God truly is, not who we want Him to be**
> 3. **Community: an understanding of how to relate to one another as Christians**
> 4. **Counsel: an ability to speak biblical truth to ourselves and to others**

Foundational to the Christian faith is the doctrine of the Trinity. The Christian faith is monotheistic—we believe in and worship the one true God. We also believe God exists in three distinct but equal Persons: Father, Son, and Holy Spirit. Once we have a basic understanding of the Trinity, we need to understand in particular, what makes Jesus unique. Today, as we consider Jesus' virgin birth, we will see that He is fully God and fully man.

Read the Apostles' Creed aloud as a group before watching the video for session 4.

WATCH

*Use this viewer guide to follow along and
take notes as you watch video session 4.*

One of the most common ways that we sin is by outright rejecting how God
designed the universe to work.

You are being discipled. Everyone is discipled by someone or something. The key
question for us is, "What story are we buying into?"

Some of us sin by using religion to not need God. We do lots of "good" religious
things as a means of convincing ourselves we don't need God.

The triune God of the universe—God the Father, God the Son, God the Holy Spirit,
three in one—is after the hearts of men.

God is an initiating God. He gets His holy hands dirty—He takes initiative to
save us.

1. SYMMETRY
God is not interested in mere action. He isn't ultimately concerned with getting us
to do the right things. He wants our hearts to delight ultimately in Him.

2. CLARITY
The message of the Bible is not that we must earn God's love but that His love is
freely offered to us. His love is freely given.

3. COMMUNITY
If we think that we are called to earn God's love, we will compete with each other
to prove that we are better than each other. If we know God's love is a gift, we will
serve and love each other out of love for God.

4. COUNSEL
Let's help each other stop trying to earn God's love and instead live in the
freedom and joy of knowing that He loves us and initiates a relationship with us.

DISCUSS

Discuss this week's video using the following questions.

READ LUKE 1:26-38.

Why is it important, not only in this story but also in our lives, to know that our God initiates a relationship with His people?

How does Mary's response reveal faith in a God who overcomes impossibilities?

When have you questioned God's work in the midst of a difficult situation? How has God proved Himself throughout Scripture?

READ ISAIAH 1:11 AND JEREMIAH 31:33.

Why did God not delight in these sacrifices (Isa. 1:11)?
What was missing?

According to Jeremiah 31:33, what is the triune God after? Why is this important to recognize?

What is the difference between trying to earn God's approval and living like you already have it?

How might we help each other live with a greater awareness of God's initiating love?

How might we help each other delight more deeply in God?

What's your primary takeaway in response to the teaching on "Who was conceived by the Holy Spirit; born of the virgin Mary"?

What other thoughts or questions do you have?

*Make time this week to complete the following
personal studies before the next group session.*

Personal Study

The presence and activity of God are established in the opening words of Scripture (see Gen. 1:1). Throughout the Bible we read of God's miraculous work as what the creed has summarized as "the Father Almighty." He's infinitely powerful, yet intensely personal.

READ EXODUS 40:34-38.

In the Old Testament the glory of the Lord was seen as a cloud that rested on the tabernacle, the portable temple of God's people, the place where they worshiped God. This visible representation of the glory of the Lord was called the *shekinah*. In Ezekiel 10 the prophet Ezekiel saw the glory of the Lord, the *shekinah*, leave the temple, but Ezekiel also had a vision of God's glory returning to a new temple, which is recorded in Ezekiel 43:1-5.

READ LUKE 1:35.

The Bible says the Holy Spirit would "overshadow" Mary in order for her to conceive a son. In the Greek translation of the Old Testament, the same word for overshadow is used to describe the cloud of God's glory in Exodus 40:35, where the Bible says, "Moses was not able to enter the tent of meeting because the cloud settled on it, and the glory of the LORD [*shekinah*] filled the tabernacle."

Luke connected the *shekinah* glory of God to the conception of Jesus. His overwhelmingly glorious presence in the tabernacle and the temple now manifested itself through Mary as she conceived, carried, and gave birth to her firstborn child, the only Son of God.

What do you think would be lost if the creed said "born of the virgin Mary?" without saying "conceived by the Holy Spirit"?

The Scriptures are full of miraculous births of people meant for a specific purpose: Sarah and Abraham had Isaac, the promised child and father of God's covenant people (see Gen. 18:9-14); Jacob and Rachel had Joseph, the royal savior (see Gen. 30:22-24); Manoah and his wife had Samson, the judge (see Judg. 13); Elkanah and Hannah had Samuel, the prophet (see 1 Sam. 1); and Zechariah and

Elizabeth had John the Baptist, the preacher of repentance and the kingdom of God (see Luke 1:5-25,57-63). In each of these cases, the Lord opened barren wombs and provided a child when none seemed possible—although the woman conceived with her husband. In each case the unexpected birth was foretold. In the Book of Isaiah, the prophet Isaiah characterized Israel as a barren woman longing for children and prophesied that she would one day be a mother (see Isa. 66:7-14).

How did each of the miraculous births in Scripture point to Jesus?

All of history had been leading up to Jesus. The opening chapter of John's Gospel uses the same language as the creation story in Genesis, words like in the beginning, light, darkness, and world. John was clearly pointing to Jesus as the Almighty, the Creator, Christ, and Lord as the only Son of God. Then John gave a beautiful picture of the supernatural birth.

READ JOHN 1:14.

The Greek word John used for dwelt means "to tabernacle." God has tabernacled with us through the birth of Jesus, making His glory known to the world.

In what ways has God made Himself known to you?

How does it change your life to know that God wants to be with you?

Prayer

Father, You're truly the God of the universe. You're so much bigger, so much more glorious than I can understand. Thank You for caring so intimately for me, even in all Your majesty, that You sent Your Son to become flesh and blood for my sake. Holy Spirit, help my heart remember and be comforted in knowing that I have a God who truly empathizes with me in every way and loves me enough to dwell with me. Amen.

In the birth of Jesus, we see God entering our world in a beautiful and unexpected way. An early church theologian named Athanasius described God's incarnation this way: "He entered the world in a new way, stooping to our level in His love and Self-revealing to us."[1]

When Athanasius said Christ stooped to our level in the incarnation, he reminded us that God condescended, voluntarily put aside His superiority, and made Himself like us in order to have communion with us. The very God of the universe humbled Himself by taking on Himself total humanity in its weakest form, a baby.

READ PHILIPPIANS 2:3-8.

Identify and list the words used to describe the humility of Christ.

Like faith, humility is ultimately demonstrated in obedience to God. Jesus humbled Himself in obedience to God. Verse 6 says He "did not count equality with God a thing to be grasped." This means Jesus didn't cling to His position of honor, holding Himself above the will of God. It wasn't beneath Him to live and die as a man even though He was and is part of the triune God.

Look at the story of Mary to see Christlike humility. To be clear, the Bible doesn't give any explanation for why God chose Mary. Like us all, she was a sinner in need of a Savior (Luke 1:47). Scripture doesn't say she was rewarded for her godliness, but we see her humble obedience demonstrated in her response to God's grace.

READ LUKE 1:26-38.

Put yourself in Mary's place. She was a young girl, most likely barely in her teens, engaged to be married, and an angel appeared to tell her that she was going to be pregnant. If that wasn't shocking enough, Mary would become pregnant while remaining a virgin, and the baby would be the Son of God. Surely no one in history had ever been more surprised.

Notice in Mary's response to the angel that she was afraid (see v. 29), she had questions (see v. 34), yet she submitted herself to God's will in humble obedience (see v. 38).

What about complete obedience to God frightens you? Explain.

What questions do you have about living by faith?

In what areas of your life are you most prone to pride?

What will you do so that Mary's words become the posture of your heart?

I am the servant of the Lord; let it be to me according to your word.
LUKE 1:38

Prayer

Holy Spirit of God, thank You for making my heart new and united with Christ. Thank You that in my union with Him, I'm reminded that You've chosen the weak things of the world, including the Messiah born of a virgin, to shame the wisdom of the wise. In the incarnation, Christ, You stooped to my level in order to reveal Yourself to me. Make me Your ambassador and proclaimer of this beautiful gospel message. Amen.

1. Saint Athanasius of Alexandria, as quoted in *Christian Doctrine,* ed. Lindsey Hall, Murray Rae, and Steven Holmes (London: SCM, 2010), 176.

Popular culture often looks down on ideas and events that seem as irrational and unbelievable as the virgin birth. Some say science and culture have progressed to a point that we can leave supernatural beliefs behind in favor of what can be proved, observed, and repeated. However, the Bible is full of miracles.

Ultimately, as a Christian, you must decide whether you believe in an almighty God who has authority and power over all things. If the God of the Bible exists, miracles are simply part of the deal; that's just part of how an almighty Creator works. It's quite logical to conclude that a supernatural God works in supernatural ways. It's His nature.

Nothing will be impossible with God.
LUKE 1:37

Do you believe these words of the angel who spoke to Mary? Why or why not?

Belief in the virgin birth is essential in shaping the Christian life. It testifies to the nature of Jesus as both God and man, as well as to the fact that we have an all-powerful Father who is active in the world He made, revealing Himself to people. And finally, it tells us that Jesus, did not inherit Adam's sin nature (Rom. 5:12-32).

Many, if not most, difficulties with or objections to believing in God are more about ourselves and our circumstances than they are about God. Take a look at the story of a father who was in a difficult situation but was learning how to believe. Then answer the following questions related to the four areas addressed in the group session.

READ MARK 9:14-29.

1. SYMMETRY

What difficult, painful, or hopeless situation are you facing that seems as if it would take a miracle to change for the better?

2. CLARITY

Just as the disciples were unable to save the boy, we're completely dependent on Jesus' miraculous work in our lives. We've already seen that Christ is the only way to experience true and eternal life. We can't be good enough, try hard enough, have good enough intentions, or know the right things to say or do to attain eternal life on our own. Salvation is the greatest miracle of all, transforming sinful people into the righteousness of Christ (see 2 Cor. 5:21). All other miracles point to the person and work of Jesus Christ.

> **How have you experienced God's work in your life to accomplish things you could never do for yourself?**

3. COMMUNITY

> **In what ways do you struggle with pessimism? How can you set an example for the people around you by believing that anything is possible with God and that no situation is hopeless?**

4. COUNSEL

> **Consider the areas of pessimism and bad attitudes in your life. In what specific ways do those attitudes reveal a lack of faith in God's ability to work in those circumstances?**

Prayer

Reflect on the confession and plea of the father in
Mark 9:24. Cry out to God, making this your prayer. Be specific
about the areas in which you need to trust Him.
I believe; help my unbelief!
MARK 9:24

Week Five

I believe in God the Father Almighty,
    Creator of heaven and earth,
And in Jesus Christ, His only Son, our Lord,
Who was conceived by the Holy Spirit;
    born of the virgin Mary;
Suffered under Pontius Pilate;
    was crucified, dead, and buried.
He descended to hell; the third day
    He rose again from the dead;
He ascended to heaven and sits on the
    right hand of the Father Almighty,
From whence He shall come to judge
    the living and the dead.
I believe in the Holy Spirit,
The holy catholic church,
    the communion of saints,
The forgiveness of sins,
The resurrection of the body,
    and the life everlasting. Amen.

𝕲𝖗𝖔𝖚𝖕 𝕾𝖙𝖚𝖉𝖞

START

SUFFERED UNDER PONTIUS PILATE; WAS CRUCIFIED, DEAD, AND BURIED

Welcome to session 5 of The Apostles' Creed.

Let's begin by taking a few minutes to review this past week.

Who is Jesus? What makes Him unique? What is the significance of His virgin birth?

Day 3 focused on the grid for understanding and applying each of the core doctrines summarized in the Apostles' Creed. Which of the four areas were most applicable this week and why? (Refer to pp. 48–49 if needed.)

1. **Symmetry: a balanced, deep understanding of the Bible**
2. **Clarity: a picture of who God truly is, not who we want Him to be**
3. **Community: an understanding of how to relate to one another as Christians**
4. **Counsel: an ability to speak biblical truth to ourselves and to others**

Last week we studied the birth of Jesus. This week we'll see why He was born: Jesus' incarnation was necessary for His crucifixion. He was born to die, but He died so that we could truly live.

Read the Apostles' Creed aloud as a group before watching the video for session 5.

WATCH

*Use this viewer guide to follow along and
take notes as you watch video session 5.*

The death of Christ reconciles us to God—Jesus died so that our sin might be forgiven and our broken relationship with God might be healed.

All our little problems with anger, jealousy, and lust are not our ultimate problem. These things are symptoms of a greater problem.

Our ultimate issue is that we were created by God to commune with Him and do life with one another and we've rejected both of these callings.

When sin entered the world, it wrecked our relationship with God and with one another.

1. SYMMETRY
The death of Jesus helps you understand how much God hates sin—all sin.

2. CLARITY
The death of Jesus solves our brokenness before God.

3. COMMUNITY
The death of Jesus also reconciles us to one another.

4. COUNSEL
- The death of Christ creates a community that is both universal and local.

- The cross is a visible picture of the love of God for you in Christ.

- The joy set before Christ in the cross was glorifying God (Heb. 12:1-2).

- You and I are the joy set before Christ on that day.

- You can stop striving and rest in the accomplished work of Jesus Christ.

DISCUSS

Discuss this week's video using the following questions.

Matt asked us to consider how we could look at the cross of Christ claim that it is beautiful. How would you answer that question?

Matt said our ultimate issue is not all our little issues with various sins like anger, jealousy, or lust. What is our ultimate issue? Why is it crucial that we not lose sight of this?

How does the death of Christ reconcile us to God? Why do we need to be reconciled to God?

READ JOHN 18:36-38.

What did Jesus say He had come into the world to do?

Why is it important that we believe that Jesus was a real person in history?

Why is it significant for the creed to emphasize the biblical account of Jesus' suffering, crucifixion, death, and burial as historical facts?

How is the cross a picture of God's love for us? How is it a picture of God's hatred of all sin? What sins do we treat as more or less hated by God?

Where would we be if Jesus hadn't suffered and died for us?

In what ways are you striving to feel lovable and worthy rather than accepting the forgiveness God offers you through Jesus?

How might you be more intentional about sharing the good news of what Jesus has done with your friends, teammates and neighbors?

Remember to complete the following personal studies before the next group session.

Personal Study

DAY 1

Suffering is an inevitable part of the human experience. The degrees of suffering might differ from person to person, but everyone experiences periods of suffering. Serious accidents, unexpected illnesses, and spiritual crises can all be causes of suffering.

Reflect on a time in your life when you or someone in your family suffered. What happened? How did you respond?

How do most people respond to suffering? What emotions, thoughts, or questions have you had when suffering?

READ ISAIAH 52:14; 53:4-5.

These verses foretell of the suffering Jesus would endure on the cross. List the words used in these verses to describe Jesus' suffering.

READ MATTHEW 27:24-26.

Pontius Pilate was governor over Judea from A.D. 26 to 36. This mention of Pilate in the Apostles' Creed may seem odd, but it highlights Christ's suffering as a historical event. The eternal Son entered our world, and a human court convicted Him of crimes He didn't commit. This event really happened. Jesus, fully human, experienced real suffering at a specific point in history.

In Christ, God has experienced true, intense suffering. What does this tell us about God? How might this realization change your perspective on the suffering you are facing or may one day face?

Why is it important for faith to be rooted in historical facts? How does it change your perspective on day-to-day events—especially in suffering—to remember what Christ has already done for you?

READ ROMANS 5:1-11.

List the words used to describe in past tense what Christ has done for you. How do Christ's past actions change your perspective on the things that are frustrating you most in your life right now?

Believing in Christ doesn't exempt you from suffering. In fact, some suffering may result because of your faith (see John 15:18-21).

What hope do you have as a Christian in the midst of suffering?

Prayer

Jesus, thank You for paying the price for my sins and for dying the death I deserve. The cross is a reminder of Your love for me. Continue to transform my life and make me more like You. I love You because You first loved me. Amen.

The crucifixion was the ultimate display of how we, as the human race, hate God's authority in our lives. Our sinful hearts rejected Christ, in spite of all His displays of love, because we hated His claim of lordship. If He's the rightful King over our lives, we must confess and repent of our rebellion and surrender our lives in submission to His rule. But instead, we demanded that Jesus be executed.

READ MATTHEW 27.

How does the crucifixion highlight the ugliness of sin? What does the crucifixion tell you about what God thinks of your sin?

In what ways are you prone to demand what you want, resisting the idea that Jesus is Lord of everything?

God wasn't surprised by the world's hatred and rejection of Jesus. And Jesus didn't suffer and die in a way that was out of His control. Before the crucifixion Jesus told His disciples:

No one takes [my life] from me, but I lay it down of my own accord.
I have authority to lay it down, and I have authority to take it up again.
JOHN 10:18

The Roman Empire asserted control through brutal practices like crucifixion, a form of execution reserved for people who posed a threat to Rome. Often the condemned were crucified along busy roads as reminders that Rome had power over life and death. But the apostle Paul said the rulers and authorities who crucified Him were put to shame (see Col. 2:13-15). Jesus' apparent defeat was a victory, and He triumphed over those who were trying to conquer Him. His willingness to suffer and die, before demonstrating authority over life and death in His resurrection, was the ultimate act of love for all people who put their faith in Jesus.

Therefore, because the Father accepted Jesus' payment for our sin, He now sees us as forgiven and justified.

READ ROMANS 3:10-26.

How does Paul describe us apart from Christ in Romans 3:10-18? Why is this important to remember?

How do these verses address both judgment and grace?

READ ROMANS 5:6-11.

List all the descriptions used for people apart from the work of Jesus.

In light of the Scriptures you've read today, emphasizing the sin and hopelessness of life apart from Christ, how can you rejoice? What does the death of Jesus make possible?

Prayer

Jesus, thank You for dying for my sins. In Your death You've reconciled me to the Father. My life is changed forever because of Your love for me. I want to be like You and live in this world in such a way that my commitment to You is evident in the way I love You and others. Please be gracious to me as I try to live to that end. Amen.

DAY 3

From the beginning of history, the consequence of sin has been death. God warned Adam that disobedience—eating the fruit—would result in inevitable death (see Gen. 2:17). The first death in the garden was an animal, sacrificed to make skins to cover Adam and Eve after they sinned. In the garden God's judgment and grace were seen in the literal covering of Adam's shame by the skin of an animal, a sacrificial death (see 3:21). Immediately following the fall of humanity, we read about the sons of Adam offering sacrifices to God and His warning about the deadly effects of sin (see 4:3-7). From the time of Adam until the time of Jesus, sacrifice was a part of the relationship between God and His people.

READ ROMANS 5:12-21.

Jesus' death and resurrection changed everything. We can now have a right relationship with God again. Our disobedience, our sin, and our rebellion as His enemies are all forgiven. No amount of right or wrong decisions, good or bad behavior could ever make us right before God. So as He did after that first sin, He stepped in, sought us, and called us to receive the sacrifice He provided. But the sacrifice of Jesus is infinitely greater than any other offering.

READ HEBREWS 10:1-10.

Based on what you've studied, including the verses from Romans 5 and Hebrews 10, why was Jesus' death on the cross necessary?

Let's look now at some ways this profound reality changes our lives. Imagine you're having a conversation with a friend. Use the following questions to help you put into your own words a gospel explanation of Jesus' crucifixion.

1. SYMMETRY

If God is a good and loving God, is sin really a big problem?

2. CLARITY

Are some sins too big for God to forgive? Explain.

3. COMMUNITY

I keep messing up no matter how hard I try to be a good person. If God takes sin so seriously, how could He ever love me?

4. COUNSEL

What do I have to do as a Christian to be forgiven of all my sins? How can I be good enough to repay God for what I've done?

Prayer

Record a prayer confessing the seriousness of your sin and admitting your personal responsibility and need for Jesus' sacrifice. Praise Him for willingly sacrificing His life in your place, setting you free from death and hopelessness.

Week Six

I believe in God the Father Almighty,
    Creator of heaven and earth,
And in Jesus Christ, His only Son, our Lord,
Who was conceived by the Holy Spirit;
    born of the virgin Mary;
Suffered under Pontius Pilate;
    was crucified, dead, and buried.
He descended to hell; the third day
    He rose again from the dead;
He ascended to heaven and sits on the
    right hand of the Father Almighty,
From whence He shall come to judge
    the living and the dead.
I believe in the Holy Spirit,
The holy catholic church,
    the communion of saints,
The forgiveness of sins,
The resurrection of the body,
    and the life everlasting. Amen.

Group Study

HE DESCENDED TO HELL; THE THIRD DAY HE ROSE AGAIN FROM THE DEAD

Welcome to session 6 of The Apostles' Creed.

Let's begin by taking a few minutes to review this past week.

> **What did Jesus accomplish for us through his suffering and death? Why is this crucial to our faith?**

> **Day 3 focused on the grid for understanding and applying each of the core doctrines summarized in the Apostles' Creed. Which of the four areas were most applicable this week and why? (Refer to pages 58–59 if needed.)**

>> 1. **Symmetry: a balanced, robust understanding of the Bible**
>> 2. **Clarity: a picture of who God truly is, not who we want Him to be**
>> 3. **Community: an understanding of how to relate to one another as Christians**
>> 4. **Counsel: an ability to speak biblical truth to ourselves and to others**

The death, burial, and resurrection of Jesus are essential beliefs, and historical events, to the Christian faith. Consequently, the Apostles' Creed once again emphasizes the fact that Jesus fully experienced death on our behalf before being raised from the dead. The inclusion of hell in the creed is controversial and debated among Christians, but we'll see why it's an important part of what we believe to be true about the gospel of Jesus Christ.

*Read the Apostles' Creed aloud as a group
before watching the video for session 6.*

WATCH

It is important for us not to turn our eyes from the suffering of Jesus Christ. In the brutality of the cross we see God's seriousness about sin.

On the cross Jesus absorbed all the sins, and all the wrath of God, of all of those who have and would trust in Christ.

Separation from God—that's the hell that Christ experiences.

Hell is the absence of the presence of God to bless and is simply the presence of God to judge.

The resurrection of Jesus Christ was a bodily, real, physical resurrection.

Because Christ is not dead, we can be sure that all our sins have been forgiven.

There will be a physical resurrection from the dead.

1. SYMMETRY
Being sealed by the Holy Spirit of God simply means that the Spirit has come to dwell in us. In other words, we are no longer separated from God—the third person of the Trinity dwells with and in us.

2. CLARITY
Through faith in Christ, we experience a spiritual resurrection. We are dead in our sins, and we are made alive in the resurrection of Christ.

3. COMMUNITY
The resurrected, bodily Jesus continues to extend the invitation to forgiveness and eternal life. We are also called to live in community, helping one another love Jesus and live for Him.

4. COUNSEL
If you have trusted Christ, you don't owe a debt to God any more. Your sin has been paid for. Let's help each other live in the freedom of having been forgiven.

DISCUSS

Discuss this week's video using the following questions.

Why is it good news that Jesus fully experienced death?

Why is it good news that Jesus was physically resurrected?

READ EPHESIANS 2:1-5

What false sense of freedom does the world pursue apart from Jesus?

How does this text describe us before Christ? What power brings destruction in our broken world and human hearts?

What does the fact that Jesus had to die tell us about God's justice? What does it tell us about the cost of sin?

How do the death and resurrection of Jesus demonstrate that God is both all powerful and all loving?

READ JAMES 5:16

If we have already been forgiven, why does James tell us to honestly confess our sins to each other?

Why do we fear confession, repentance, and honesty? Why must these always be a part of our Christian walk?

What is your reaction to Matt's description of the phrase "He descended to hell?" How does this phrase give weight to our own sinfulness?

What's your primary takeaway in response to the teaching on *He descended to hell, the third day He rose again from the dead?*

Remember to complete the following personal studies before the next group session.

Personal Study

DAY 1

Let's go ahead and address the elephant in the room: the phrase "He descended to hell" is controversial. This phrase wasn't included in the earliest forms of the Apostles' Creed but was added by a Roman theologian named Rufinus in A.D. 390.

Rufinus didn't interpret the phrase to mean that Jesus went to a place of eternal judgment but rather that Jesus went down into the earth and was buried. Christ, in His humanity, fully experienced death on our behalf. He willingly put Himself forward to be judged in our place for our sins. Jesus descended into the grave, into the earth He created. By doing so, Jesus experienced death with us and for us. He also defeated death for us and was resurrected, as we will be someday if we know Christ as Savior and Lord.

READ MATTHEW 12:38-40.

What did Jesus say would be the great sign or miracle proving that He was the only Son of God?

Why does it matter that Jesus fully experienced death and the grave for us and because of us?

How would your understanding of the gospel change if Jesus hadn't personally taken on our punishment by going to the place of death for us?

READ 1 CORINTHIANS 15:12-19.

What did Paul say about the relationship between the resurrection of Jesus and the resurrection of all people? Can you believe in one but not the other? Why or why not?

If there were no forgiveness of sin and eternal life, but believing in Jesus still made us better moral people, what did Paul conclude about such a faith (see v. 19)? What did he mean?

READ 1 CORINTHIANS 15:20-23.

The Bible often uses agricultural terms such as *firstfruits,* a word that describes the part of the harvest that's offered in thanks to God for His provision. When wheat begins to ripen in a field, it signals that soon the whole harvest will be ready.

What did Paul mean when He said Jesus is the firstfruits of the resurrection (see v. 20)?

What is Paul's conclusion, based on the fact that Jesus was resurrected?

Prayer

Father, thank You for sending Jesus to die for my sins, to descend into the grave where I deserve to be because of my sin. Thank You for raising Him from the dead, thereby proving that He's Your eternal Son; that my sins have been paid for; and that He's the righteous Messiah, sent to show me the way to eternal life. Holy Spirit, remind my heart of these truths and remind me that one day, like my Savior, Jesus Christ, I'll be bodily raised as well. I ask this in Jesus' name. Amen.

Socrates once said, "Death may be the greatest of all human blessings."[1] He meant death brings peace from the suffering of human life. But is this true? Death is normal, but is death good or even natural?

Death isn't part of the purpose we were created for. The benefit of death, such as getting to be with Jesus, is good but not death itself. Humans were made to live with God forever and not to die. Death is a curse. All of us, as descendants of Adam and Eve, have been affected by the curse of death.

Think about ways death has affected you or your family. Whom have you lost? How does the gospel give us hope in the face of death?

How does the reality of heaven, hell, and the resurrection affect your thoughts and feelings about death? How does it affect your sense of urgency in sharing the gospel?

Identify people you know who need to respond in faith to the life, death, and resurrection of Jesus Christ?

READ 2 CORINTHIANS 5.

What perspective did Paul have on our purpose in life?

Biblically, the first step of faith and obedience in the Christian life is one marked by death. We join every believer since Pentecost by identifying with Christ and one another through baptism (see Acts 2:41). As Paul wrote, "The old has passed away; behold, the new has come" (2 Cor. 5:17). Baptism is a public statement of identity—when someone is baptized, that person is claiming to belong to Christ.

It is a picture of being fully united with Christ in His death and descent into the grave, and then follows His subsequent resurrection with a new body.

READ ROMANS 6:1-11.

What's the significance of Paul's words "We were buried therefore with him" and "We too might walk in newness of life" (v. 4)? How does the resurrection change the way you live day-to-day?

When were you baptized? Describe the experience and the significance of your baptism to someone this week.

If your baptism was an identification with Christ, dying to your sin and receiving new life in Him, share that good news with someone. If you haven't been baptized or if you've been baptized but weren't sure what it meant or still have questions, be sure to speak to your leader or someone in your group.

Prayer

Father, I hate death. I love Your original creation that had no stain, no blemish, no sickness, and no death. I praise You because in Christ death has been defeated, and life is now victorious. I adore You, Son of God, who in Your death and resurrection defeated the last enemy—death. Death has literally been left in the grave. I adore You because in Your resurrection You teach me that one day my body that currently suffers will one day be perfect again. Give me faith and perseverance to long for Your return. I'm waiting for You, Jesus. Come make all things right again by the power of the Spirit. I ask these things in the name of Jesus. Amen.

1. Socrates, as quoted on Thinkexist.com [online, cited 5 December 2016]. Available from the Internet: *thinkexist.com.*

The resurrection truly makes the Christian faith unique. Throughout history many people have died for their beliefs—willingly and even eagerly giving their lives for their faith, refusing to compromise their convictions because they were certain the reward for faithfulness was greater than any suffering they endured. The difference between Jesus and any guru, prophet, teacher, leader, or hero is that He was the only Son of God and didn't stay dead. Jesus not only suffered and died but also rose from His burial place, left the tomb empty, and appeared before hundreds of eyewitnesses.

The resurrection of Jesus is not only miraculous but also evidence that He alone has authority over life and death and the ability to forgive sin. Because Christ isn't dead, we can be confident that all our sins have been forgiven.

How do these truths strengthen your faith and make Christianity unique?

READ 1 CORINTHIANS 15:3-11.

Why did Paul record different witnesses to the resurrection at different times? Why is it significant that over five hundred people saw Jesus at the same time?

Paul said some of the witnesses had fallen asleep—this was a common phrase that indicated that they had died but that death was not the end for them.

READ ISAIAH 26:19 AND DANIEL 12:2.

What do these verses say about physical death? About eternity?

One of the great but overlooked promises of the Christian faith is the fact that eternal life isn't just a spiritual reality; it's a physical reality. Believers in Christ can look forward to their resurrections and renewed bodies.

Jesus promises us a resurrection like His: renewed, eternal bodies free from weakness, suffering, and death. What areas of your life are you most looking forward to Christ bringing new life?

When we affirm the words of the Apostles' Creed, we embrace the difficult reality of death and the promise of resurrection. In the words "He descended into hell, the third day He rose again from the dead" we gain an eternal perspective. Let's reflect on our four points of perspective as we pray.

Prayer

1. SYMMETRY

Pray that God will help you live in the freedom of knowing that your eternal salvation has been secured through the death and resurrection of Jesus Christ.

2. CLARITY

Thank God that Jesus laid down His life for you, fully experiencing life, death, and becoming your sin so that you could be made new in His righteousness.

3. COMMUNITY

Ask God for opportunities to encourage others in their faith and to invite people to join the family of God through faith in His only Son—our Savior and Lord.

4. COUNSEL

Continually remind yourself of the gospel. Confess any and all sin and repent, putting off the old self and putting on the new self by the grace of Jesus Christ.

Week Seven

I believe in God the Father Almighty,
    Creator of heaven and earth,
And in Jesus Christ, His only Son, our Lord,
Who was conceived by the Holy Spirit;
    born of the virgin Mary;
Suffered under Pontius Pilate;
    was crucified, dead, and buried.
He descended to hell; the third day
    He rose again from the dead;
He ascended to heaven and sits on the
    right hand of the Father Almighty,
From whence He shall come to judge
    the living and the dead.
I believe in the Holy Spirit,
The holy catholic church,
    the communion of saints,
The forgiveness of sins,
The resurrection of the body,
    and the life everlasting. Amen.

Group Study

HE ASCENDED TO HEAVEN AND SITS ON THE RIGHT HAND OF THE FATHER ALMIGHTY

Welcome to session 7 of The Apostles' Creed.

Let's begin by taking a few minutes to review this past week.

What was the most meaningful or challenging part of your personal study from *He descended to hell, the third day He rose again from the dead*? What did you learn or experience in a specific way this week?

Day 3 used our grid for understanding and applying each of the core doctrines summarized in the Apostles' Creed as a guide for prayer. Which of the four areas were most applicable this week and why? (Refer to pp. 68–69 if needed.)

1. **Symmetry: a balanced, robust understanding of the Bible**
2. **Clarity: a picture of who God truly is, not who we want Him to be**
3. **Community: an understanding of how to relate to one another as Christians**
4. **Counsel: an ability to speak biblical truth to ourselves and to others**

Jesus not only rose from the grave, conquering sin and the power of hell; our Lord ascended (rose) into heaven. He not only fully experienced death, as we saw last week; He also has full authority over life as our sovereign King.

Read the Apostles' Creed aloud as a group before watching the video for session 7.

WATCH

*Use this viewer guide to follow along and
take notes as you watch video session 7.*

Christians have no Mecca. There is no place we must go to experience the power and presence of God.

The Holy Spirit is now the presence of Christ everywhere, available to all at any given moment.

It's not that we don't enter difficulty but that in difficulty Christ is there—His presence and power are there to transform us and turn us and change us from one degree of glory to the next.

In other words, Christ has given us the Spirit to empower us to grow to be more like Him.

I am not yet where I will be.

I am not yet what I will be.

Holy discontentment is "If Christ is an exhaustible well, then I want more."

1. SYMMETRY
Some of us need the type of holy discontentment that would make us more serious about sin and more hungry for righteousness.

2. CLARITY
The reason Christ's ascension into heaven is so beautiful is because it assures us that we have not been abandoned. We are not left to ourselves. He empowers us.

3. COMMUNITY
We are not yet what we will be. Let's help each other believe that the Spirit is at work in our lives to help us grow to live more like Jesus.

4. COUNSEL
In group life and in community life, you'll be surprised at how often it is your weaknesses that encourage and stir up faith in your brothers and sisters.

DISCUSS

Discuss the video using the following questions.

READ ACTS 1:1-11.

What did the ascension, another historical fact, reveal to Jesus' disciples?

What specific instructions did Jesus give to the disciples? How do these instructions apply to us today?

What did Matt mean when he used the term *holy discontentment*?

On a scale of 1-10 (1 being not at all and 10 being wholeheartedly), how seriously do you take sin in your life? How hungry are you for righteousness? Explain your answers.

What would it take for you to increase your desire for righteousness instead of for sin?

How can we be more aware of Christ's presence in our lives even though we do not physically see Him?

Jesus promised that He has not abandoned us. In what way is the ascension a turning point in the life of the church? Why did Jesus say His ascension benefits His followers?

What comfort is there in the statement: *we are not yet what we will be*?

When have you been encouraged by knowing you weren't the only person who has had certain thoughts or experiences? Who may need encouragement from you, knowing your past or present weaknesses?

Remember to make time this week to complete the following personal studies before the next group session.

Personal Study

This portion of the creed invites us to consider the identity of Jesus as our ascended Lord who, from His exalted position at the Father's right hand, is ruling all things.

READ ACTS 1:1-11.

How did Jesus and the two angels in white robes direct the disciples' attention to their present responsibilities?

Why would Jesus present Himself alive before promising the Holy Spirit and commissioning the disciples to be witnesses of the gospel?

As gloriously expressed by this Scripture passage and this section of the creed, the ascension confirms that Jesus is no longer among the dead and never will be again. His power has proved to be greater than anything in this world—even death. The gospel of Jesus and salvation from sin are certain for people who believe in Him.

READ ACTS 2:32-38.

As Peter preached the first Christian sermon, he concluded with the fact that Jesus rose from the dead, ascended into heaven, and sent His Holy Spirit.

God had made it known through Scripture, through His Son, and now through His Spirit that Jesus is the Messiah promised by the Old Testament prophets and the reigning Lord of all creation. This passage teaches us that as Jesus sits at the right hand of the Father, He sends or pours out the Holy Spirit. The biblical account of Jesus' ascension into heaven is meant to give us certainty.

What phrases in this passage emphasize Jesus' authority? Identify each phrase and briefly explain what it communicates.

How do these prophecies and testimonies give you confidence?

Although Jesus ascended into heaven, it is wrong to say that He is not active in the world. In reading the Book of Acts, we see numerous occasions in which Jesus was still working in the world.

Throughout the Book of Acts and the New Testament as a whole, the Holy Spirit is always mentioned when Christians are empowered as witnesses of Jesus. We've received the Spirit in order to know God and to make Him known with boldness.

Like the disciples who were looking into heaven after Jesus' ascension, what do you need to do right now to obey Jesus and to be His witness?

Prayer

Father, I pray to You in the power of the name of the Lord Jesus Christ, who's at Your right hand at this very moment. I praise Your Son because You've exalted Him above all things and because He rules and reigns over all things. I worship and exalt Your Son because He's worthy. I look forward to the day when You'll send Him to us again, and everyone in heaven and on earth will confess that He's Lord. Amen.

We often hear about what Jesus has done and what He's going to do; however, it's easy to forget about Jesus' current role in heaven.

It's vital to keep at the forefront of our hearts and minds what He has done. That's the cornerstone of the gospel as we've studied in previous weeks. But we also have a future hope that's certain. We'll look more at the future judgment and the reign of Christ in coming sessions. But don't rush past who Christ is right now and what that means for our lives today.

READ HEBREWS 7:23-28.

Verse 25 says Jesus makes intercession for us. Because Jesus ascended to the Father, He speaks to the Father on our behalf as our High Priest. This is why Christians pray in the name of Jesus. We approach God the Father with confidence through Jesus, our intercessor.

Write a definition of *intercession,* either in your own words or from a dictionary. Describe how Jesus' intercession applies to your relationship with God.

Robert Murray McCheyne, a 19th century minister in the Church of Scotland, once said, "If I could hear Christ praying for me in the next room, I would not fear a million enemies. Yet distance makes no difference; he is praying for me."

How does the knowledge that Christ is praying for you personally give you hope and confidence?

READ ROMANS 8:26-28.

When have you felt at a total loss to express your thoughts, feelings, or needs?

In what specific areas of your life are you glad to know Christ and His Spirit are interceding on your behalf?

An implication of being at the Father's right hand is that Jesus has unique authority and a unique relationship with the Father, one that belongs only to the Son. He shares in all His Father's power and authority. His presence with the Father doesn't make Him absent from the world but uniquely powerful and present by His Spirit.

READ ROMANS 8:9-17.

The Holy Spirit is present and active not only in the world around you but also in you. God the Father, Son, and Holy Spirit is not only sovereign and in control of all things, but He's also making Himself and His will known to you—His child. You've been created and redeemed for greater things than the temporary things of the flesh. God knows your deepest desires and needs, and He perfectly satisfies every one. He's good, and He's with you all the time.

Prayer

Father, I come to You in the name of Your Son, who's exalted with You in glory and majesty. Thank You for making a way for me to approach Your holy presence. There's no other way into Your presence than through Your Son. I love Him because You've given all things over to His sovereign reign and dominion, for all things were created through Him and for Him. Thank You for giving me such a great High Priest who can sympathize with me and intercede for me. I ask that You won't delay in sending Him back to His people, for the sake of our joy and Your glory. I ask all these things in His beautiful name and by the Spirit whom He has generously and abundantly poured out on me. Amen.

1. Robert Murray McCheyne, *The Works of Robert Murray McCheyne* (New York: Robert Carter & Brothers, 1874), 138.

One way you can know Jesus is alive and well is that you can meet and know Him. Or course, if you're in Christ, you already know this.

Athanasius, a fourth-century Christian theologian, wrote, "We are agreed that a dead person can do nothing: yet the Saviour works mightily every day, drawing men to religion, persuading them to virtue, teaching them about immortality, quickening their thirst for heavenly things, revealing the knowledge of the Father, inspiring strength in face of death, manifesting Himself to each, and displacing the irreligion of idols." He concluded that the conversion of a sinner is "the work of One Who lives, not of one dead; and, more than that, it is the work of God."[1] In other words, because Jesus rose from the dead, we can have confidence that He has the power to help us grow to be more like Him.

READ ACTS 9:1-9.

Can people see a noticeable difference between who you are and the world or between who you are and who you once were? Explain.

Though your testimony may not seem as dramatic as Saul's, it is no less miraculous. Describe that experience.

Has the reality of who Jesus is transformed your life? How so? Be specific.

Now let's look back at this week's study through the Apostles Creed Grid.

1. SYMMETRY

The fact that Jesus ascended into heaven and sits at the right hand of the Father Almighty should give you confidence and a sense of holy discontentment, a refusal to settle for anything less than a life that glorifies the risen Lord.

2. CLARITY

You don't have to (and you can't) live the Christian life by your own strength. Your abilities have no effect on the righteousness of Christ and on your mission to be His witness. You live in His power. He's interceding on your behalf.

3. COMMUNITY

The living God, Jesus Christ, changed Saul's life. He can change anything in your life too. That also means He can change anybody around you, no matter how deeply entrenched in sin they may be. Because you can be sure that Jesus is alive and in control, you can have confidence that He's at work in and through you. You aren't yet what you'll be. He's not finished with you. He has made Himself known to you and is working through you as His witness.

4. COUNSEL

When you fall into temptation, don't give in to the paralysis of guilt and shame. You'll be surprised by how often your weaknesses can encourage and stir up the faith of your brothers and sisters in Christ. Allow God's radical work in your life—including your past sin and current struggles—to testify of the worthiness and power of Jesus Christ. Your Lord ever reigns at the right hand of the Father in heaven.

Prayer

Thank God that Jesus is alive and in control, seated at His right hand with all authority. Pray for boldness to testify of His worthiness in your life.

1. St. Athanasius, *On the Incarnation,* trans. a religious of CSMV (Crestwood, NY: St. Vladimir's Seminary Press, 1944), 61–62.

Week Eight

I believe in God the Father Almighty,
  Creator of heaven and earth,
And in Jesus Christ, His only Son, our Lord,
Who was conceived by the Holy Spirit;
  born of the virgin Mary;
Suffered under Pontius Pilate;
  was crucified, dead, and buried.
He descended to hell; the third day
  He rose again from the dead;
He ascended to heaven and sits on the
  right hand of the Father Almighty,
From whence He shall come to judge
  the living and the dead.
I believe in the Holy Spirit,
The holy catholic church,
  the communion of saints,
The forgiveness of sins,
The resurrection of the body,
  and the life everlasting. Amen.

Group Study

START

FROM WHENCE HE SHALL COME TO JUDGE THE LIVING AND THE DEAD

Welcome to session 8 of The Apostles' Creed.

Let's begin by taking a few minutes to review this past week.

> **What is the significance of Christ's ascension into heaven? Why is this good news for us?**

> **Day 3 focused on the grid for understanding and applying the core doctrines summarized in the Apostles' Creed. Which of the four areas were most applicable this week and why? (Refer to pp. 78–79 if needed.)**

> 1. **Symmetry: a balanced, deep understanding of the Bible**
> 2. **Clarity: a picture of who God truly is, not who we want Him to be**
> 3. **Community: an understanding of how to relate to one another as Christians**
> 4. **Counsel: an ability to speak biblical truth to ourselves and to others**

One thing that Christians today seem to forget or neglect is the fact that Jesus not only rose from the dead and ascended to heaven, but He's also coming back. His return is something that, when kept in our hearts and minds, will transform our daily lives. He will return. When He returns, everyone will give an account for their lives and for how they've responded to the gospel.

Read the Apostles' Creed aloud as a group
before watching the video for session 8.

WATCH

*Use this viewer guide to follow along and
take notes as you watch video session 8.*

What's revealed in the return of Christ is His glory.

There's a day coming on which all the nations and all the angels will sit around His glorious throne, and no one will dispute in that moment that He's King.

On that day, there will not be a debate about whether Jesus is who He says He is.

Jesus says that "I the Shepherd, I the Son of Man, I the King, will step in, and I'll separate the sheep from the goats."

The King who is the Judge, who is sitting in glory on His throne, associates Himself with the lowly.

1. SYMMETRY
We have a just and merciful Judge. He must judge sin but He offers mercy to all who trust in Christ's death and resurrection.

2. CLARITY
Christ is both sovereign King and merciful Savior. He is both the one who will judge but also the means by which we can stand in the day of judgment.

3. COMMUNITY
The reality that Jesus is both our merciful Savior and our just judge should give weight to our daily lives and actions.

Let's help each other submit to the King and live for His glory.

4. COUNSEL
Knowing that Jesus is both the just judge and merciful Savior should move us to be serious about the proclamation of the Kingdom.

DISCUSS

Discuss the video using the following questions.

READ 2 TIMOTHY 4:1-2.

Why would judgment be given in this text as the reason for preaching, teaching, and making disciples of Jesus through the gospel?

Do you typically think of God as looking to give mercy or as being right to judge sin? What's the danger of thinking of Him as either exclusively just or merciful?

Other than salvation, how have you specifically experienced God's mercy?

Are you more likely to desire God to be just or merciful to other people?

How does the fact that Christ takes no pleasure in the destruction of the wicked affect the way you view others? The way you view God?

Why is it important to mourn and to celebrate with believers, even those whom we will never see in this life?

Knowing that judgment is a reality for all people, who do you know that needs to hear the gospel of our merciful King? How will we hold each other accountable to share the urgent news of salvation by faith alone?

What's your primary takeaway in response to the teaching on *from whence He shall come to judge the living and the dead*?

What other thoughts or questions do you have?

Take time this week to complete the following personal studies before the next group session.

Personal Study

DAY 1

This week's portion of the creed closes out the part dealing with the person and work of Jesus. Having described Jesus' past and present ministry, this phrase describes His future work. These words direct our attention to Jesus' return. Remember what was said to the disciples on the Mount of Olives? The ascension was not only proof of Jesus' authority, but also a promise of His return.

READ ACTS 1:6-11.

Why would Jesus' return be promised at the moment of His ascension?

What do Jesus' past ascension to heaven and His future return from heaven have to do with our present life on earth?

To understand the purpose of our lives and what it means to be witnesses (see Acts 1:8), it's important to consider the meaning and purpose of Jesus' coming.

READ HEBREWS 9:27-28.

With regard to believers, what was the purpose of Jesus' first coming?

What will be the purpose of His second coming?

Only a handful of disciples witnessed the Lord ascend into heaven. His birth was even less conspicuous. Even with a sky full of angels singing, Jesus' coming into the world was witnessed only by Mary, Joseph, and a few shepherds. However, His second coming will be unlike His first.

READ REVELATION 1:4-8.

What names and phrases are ascribed to Jesus? What do they emphasize?

Who will witness the second coming? How will those witnesses respond?

Rate how often you think about the fact that Jesus will return. Use a circle for your answer.

1	2	3	4	5	6	7	8	9	10
Never									Constantly

Using the same scale, how would you rank your belief that Jesus will physically return to earth? Use a square for your answer.

Consider your answers to the two previous questions and compare the rankings marked by the circle and the square. What do your two scores reveal about your belief that Jesus could return any day—even today?

Why does it matter whether we believe Jesus will return?

Prayer

Heavenly Father, teach me to hope in the return of Jesus. Show me how to walk in wisdom as someone who expects to stand before Him, not to be punished but to give an account for my joyful obedience. Thank You that His return means the end of sin and suffering. In Jesus' name, amen.

DAY 2

Although it hasn't happened yet, the second coming of Jesus is just as certain as the first coming.

The question to ask yourself isn't whether He will return, because He will. The question to ask yourself isn't even a matter of when He will return, because we can't know. The only question you need to ask yourself is whether you're ready to stand before Him when He returns to judge the living and the dead.

READ MATTHEW 24:36-44.

The Bible teaches us that we can't know when Jesus will return and that we shouldn't waste time wondering but should always be ready.

Why did Jesus emphasize that nobody knows when He will return?

What would change if you knew Jesus would return this week?

I would ...

I would not ...

If you would change something because you knew the time of Jesus' return, what keeps you from making those changes in your life now?

Read the following parables and summarize key points in each.

Matthew 24:45-51

Matthew 25:1-13

Matthew 25:14-30

Matthew 25:31-46

Are the imagery and intensity of Jesus' stories surprising to you? What do they reveal about the nature of His return?

Based on the previous parables, what does it look like to eagerly anticipate Jesus' return? Explain.

Prayer

Thank God for His justice and mercy. Ask Him for a spirit of anticipation as you eagerly watch for His return and make the most of every opportunity to share the gospel and to treat each day as if it could be your last opportunity to show Christ's love to the world.

DAY 3

Most of the time we don't like to think about God's judgment. Unless we're seeking comfort in the fact that God will judge blatantly wicked people, we prefer to dwell on the God who "so loved the world, that he gave his only Son" (John 3:16). The grace of God through the sacrificial death of Jesus is indeed unique among major religions throughout history, but it's also because God is holy and good that He judges sin with incredible wrath.

The gospel is good news because without faith in Jesus, we would all rightfully receive the punishment we deserve for our sin. For those who belong to Christ, though, He has taken the punishment of death and God's wrath on Himself. But for those who haven't placed their faith in Jesus, refusing to bow their knee to Him as Lord, they'll receive the judgment they're due.

READ ROMANS 14:11-12.

How does giving an account for ourselves relate to praying and confessing Jesus as Lord?

People today debate religious beliefs or ignore Jesus altogether. They may view Him in various ways, some even positive, but the truth will be made clear in the end. There will be a day when all the nations and all the angels will sit around His glorious throne, and no one will dispute that He is King.

As we all give an account for every single thing we've done, there's no amount of good that will outweigh the bad—not for any of us. Justice will be served, and all sin will be accounted for. Ultimately, Jesus is the only reason we don't stand condemned in the sight of God. It was Jesus who completely took on our sin and paid the price in full, nailing our certificate of debt to His cross (see Col. 2:13-14).

READ REVELATION 20:11-15.

What does God promise to do in the end according to these verses?

The incomparable beauty of the gospel is that the King, who's also the Judge, sitting in glory on His throne, associates Himself with the lowly and saves us.

Prayer

1. SYMMETRY

Take a moment to let the weight of eternal judgment sink in. You'll stand before God's throne to give an account for everything. That's a reality. Thank God that He's a just Judge who's right to punish sin and that you've been declared innocent because you stand in Christ and not on your own merits.

2. CLARITY

Ask God to break your heart over sin and to give you a burden to see people saved rather than judged. Keep in mind that Christ takes no pleasure in the destruction of the wicked (see Ezek. 33:11). He gave His only Son to die for us while we were still His enemies so that we could be made righteous in His sight (see Rom. 5:8).

3. COMMUNITY

Pray for the gospel to spread to every tribe, tongue, and nation. Pray for brothers and sisters in Christ throughout the world who are being persecuted.

4. COUNSEL

Pray for faithful endurance in the midst of all circumstances. Ask God to help you and your brothers and sisters in Christ keep your hope fixed on Jesus, knowing that in the end every knee will bow and every tongue confess that He is Lord (see Phil. 2:10-11).

Week Nine

I believe in God the Father Almighty,
    Creator of heaven and earth,
And in Jesus Christ, His only Son, our Lord,
Who was conceived by the Holy Spirit;
    born of the virgin Mary;
Suffered under Pontius Pilate;
    was crucified, dead, and buried.
He descended to hell; the third day
    He rose again from the dead;
He ascended to heaven and sits on the
    right hand of the Father Almighty,
From whence He shall come to judge
    the living and the dead.
I believe in the Holy Spirit,
The holy catholic church,
    the communion of saints,
The forgiveness of sins,
The resurrection of the body,
    and the life everlasting. Amen.

𝕲𝔯𝔬𝔲𝔭 𝔖𝔱𝔲𝔡𝔶

START

I BELIEVE IN THE HOLY SPIRIT

Welcome to session 9 of The Apostles' Creed.

Let's begin by taking a few minutes to review this past week.

Why must we believe that Jesus is coming back? What will Jesus do when He returns? How should His return give us hope, confidence, and purpose in the things we do every day?

Day 3 used our grid for understanding and applying each of the core doctrines summarized in the Apostles' Creed as a guide for prayer. Which of the four areas were most applicable this week and why? (Refer to pages 88–89 if needed.)

1. **Symmetry: a balanced, robust understanding of the Bible**
2. **Clarity: a picture of who God truly is, not who we want Him to be**
3. **Community: an understanding of how to relate to one another as Christians**
4. **Counsel: an ability to speak biblical truth to ourselves and to others**

The Apostles' Creed may seem to take a sudden turn in its train of thought this week, but it backtracks a bit to fill in the gap between Jesus' ascension in the past and His return in the future. What do we do now in the meantime? While Christ is seated at the right hand of God, the Holy Spirit is active and present in each of His people as we speak. In fact, it is by the Spirit that we can understand and apply what we are about to study and discuss.

Read the Apostles' Creed aloud as a group
before watching the video for session 9.

WATCH

The solution to our sin problem and our separation from God is solved in the adopting work of the Holy Spirit through the life, death, and resurrection of Jesus Christ.

The gospel promises us that God will not leave us as spiritual orphans.

Being a son or daughter of God, being adopted into the family of God, becomes an identity marker that nothing and no one can take from me.

This is what the Spirit of God does: ransoms us out of being spiritual orphans; pulls us into the household of faith; and gives us a marker of being known, loved, provided for, cared for, and pursued.

We're not obedient in order to be loved, but we are loved, and we understand love, and that love drives obedience.

The higher the love, the greater the capacity for self-sacrifice, for suffering, and ultimately for discipline.

The Holy Spirit informs and stirs up adoration that drives our obedience.

The people of God are prone to forget the faithfulness of God yesterday and simply complain about what they don't have today.

The peace that the world tries to bring isn't built in reality. The world can't keep its promises for us to actually walk in peace.

All who are led by the Spirit of God are called sons of God.

Where is the Spirit of God leading you? Where are the places in which fear is stopping you from being obedient to that leading?

DISCUSS

Discuss this week's video using the following questions.

READ ROMANS 8:14-15.

What confidence does it give you to be adopted by the Father Almighty? What comfort does it give you to be able to call Him *Abba*?

Why did Matt say that our natural desire to belong is a gift of God's grace?

In what ways, good or bad, do people seek to belong to something greater than themselves? Where have you looked for or experienced belonging?

How would you explain the difference between an obedience driven by a desire to be lovable and an obedience driven by knowing that we're already loved? What does a lack of obedience to Jesus reveal?

READ JOHN 14:23-26.

What is one of the primary roles of the Holy Spirit according to Jesus? What does this look like in our daily lives?

How are knowledge, love, and obedience related?

What did Matt mean when he said that it was blasphemous to minimize the Spirit as merely the giver of spiritual gifts?

What's your primary takeaway in response to the teaching on *I believe in the Holy Spirit*?

What other thoughts or questions do you have?

Don't forget to complete the following personal studies before the next group session.

DAY 1

Christians believe God is the Trinity. We've already seen that God has eternally existed as one essence and three distinct persons: God the Father, God the Son, and God the Holy Spirit. Each of the three persons of the Godhead is fully God, yet there's one God. The Apostles' Creed affirms the trinitarian formula when it affirms belief in the Holy Spirit.

The following passage describes each person of the Trinity.

READ JOHN 16:7-15.

Why did Jesus tell His disciples that it was to their advantage for Him to go away—ascend into heaven—and for them to have the Spirit instead?

How did Jesus refer to the Holy Spirit? What do the names suggest?

According to Jesus, what would the Spirit do? Be specific.

Sometimes people speak of the Holy Spirit in impersonal terms. In contrast, Jesus referred to the Spirit as He (a person), Helper, and Guide. The Spirit is never an it.

Why is it essential that we speak of the Holy Spirit in personal terms?

The Bible testifies that no one can know Christ except by the Holy Spirit. Therefore, the Spirit is known as the One who gives life (see John 6:63).

READ JOHN 3:1-8.

We get the phrase *born-again Christian* from Jesus' words in John 3:3. To be a part of God's eternal family, to live forever in His heavenly kingdom, we must be born again. The Greek word *anōthen,* translated here as "again," can also be translated as "from above." In other words, verses 3 and 5 are clear that spiritual life requires spiritual birth.

Have you been born again, born from above, born of the Holy Spirit? How do you know you've received the gift of life from the Spirit?

READ EPHESIANS 1:3-10.

When the Father gives you the Holy Spirit, you also receive all of Christ's benefits of sonship. Your personal relationship with Christ, your right standing before God, your spiritual growth, your adoption into God's family, and the promise of your future resurrection are all given to you by Christ through the Holy Spirit. Salvation, from beginning to end, is a gift from God the Father, accomplished by God the Son, and given through God the Holy Spirit.

How does each member of the Trinity's role in our salvation encourage you? Why is it important to realize that salvation is a gift?

Prayer

Father, thank You for drawing me by Your Holy Spirit to your beautiful Son.
The indwelling presence of the Spirit gives me more joy and peace than
anything this world could provide. Please help me walk in accordance
with the Spirit and not the flesh, for the Spirit is worthy of all honor and
praise. Thank You for the gift of knowing You through Your Holy Spirit.

DAY 2

The Holy Spirit is specifically mentioned in the Apostles' Creed because the Bible teaches that the Spirit isn't the Father, nor is He the Son, yet He's fully God. Because the Spirit is fully God and God is personal, the Spirit has personal attributes, and He acts personally. In other words, the Spirit cares about us and is intimately involved in our lives.

READ JOHN 14:26 AND 1 JOHN 2:18-27.

According to these two texts, what does the Holy Spirit teach us?

It's vital for believers to be able to tell spiritual truth from lies. One job of the Holy Spirit is to help us read and understand the Bible. This doctrine is called illumination. Illumination means God must enlighten the human mind in order for us to understand the things of God. The Spirit renews our minds and restores our senses by revealing and helping us understand spiritual truth.

READ 1 CORINTHIANS 2:10-16.

What does verse 14 say about a person's natural ability to comprehend spiritual truth?

Is this passage encouraging, discouraging, or both? Explain.

What does it mean to read the Bible with the mind of Christ?

While the Holy Spirit works in accordance with the Father and the Son to bring about salvation in the lives of believers, the Spirit also enables us to live as Christians according to His power.

READ GALATIANS 5:16-24.

According to Paul, all virtue is born of the Holy Spirit, and all evil is born of the flesh.

From which failings of the flesh do you seek the Spirit's help to be free?

How do you seek the Holy Spirit's power in resisting selfishness?

What specific fruit of the Spirit have you noticed most evidently in your life since you've known Christ?

What fruit of the Spirit, with God's help and power, would you like to exhibit more in your life?

Prayer

God, I give You all honor and praise. Have mercy on me. Give me a humble heart. Holy Spirit, help me never lose sight of the person and work of Jesus Christ. Illumine and enlighten my mind to spiritual things. Reveal to me the beautiful truth of Scripture. Lead me out of darkness and into the way of Christ. Make me a faithful, righteous person known by faith, hope, and love. Spirit of God, never let me depart from the truth that You teach me in Christ. Preserve me forever in my love for the Savior. I ask these things in the name of Jesus the Christ, my Lord and King. Amen.

DAY 3

The Spirit of God literally changes everything about your life. He ransoms you, saving you from being a spiritual orphan; bringing you into the household of faith; and marking you as a son or a daughter of God who's known, loved, provided for, cared for and pursued. Being adopted into the family of God is an identity marker that nothing and no one can take from you. Through faith in the Son, by the grace of the Father, you're a Spirit-filled member of His family.

READ JOHN 15:26 AND ACTS 2:1-4.

The Father and the Son sent the Holy Spirit to the church in one of the most climactic events in salvation history—Pentecost. The Spirit was poured out on the church as a gift from the Father and the Son. The triune God began a new work of creation. He made us new—a new Spirit-born people—the church—characterized by the indwelling presence of the Holy Spirit.

In what way is the gift of the Holy Spirit greater than any other gift we could receive, even from God?

The Holy Spirit indwells believers in the church and uniquely gives them and the church the gift of discerning and receiving the truth about God (see 1 John 1:1-3; 4:6) and rejecting false teaching (see 4:1). The Spirit unites believers and causes us to abide in Christ. The Spirit also fills us and gives us Christlike character that's powerfully and beautifully different from the way we once lived according to the flesh.

Read 2 Timothy 1:7. In what ways is fear the opposite of power, love, and self-control?

In what areas of your life can the Holy Spirit help you live with greater power, love, and self-control?

The Holy Spirit is now the presence of Christ everywhere, available to all believers at any given moment. Now, with the Holy Spirit, humans are turned into proper vessels for cosmic renewal. Let this awesome reality sink in as you use the four areas of our theological grid to guide your time of reflection and prayer.

1. SYMMETRY

How does the Holy Spirit give believers a robust understanding of the Bible?

2. CLARITY

Why would you have an incomplete understanding of who God is without a right belief in the Holy Spirit? Who is the Holy Spirit?

3. COMMUNITY

How does the Holy Spirit provide unity among fellow believers in Christ?

4. COUNSEL

What truth has the Holy Spirit impressed on you, illuminating your mind as you've studied this week's lessons? How can you rely on the Holy Spirit when you counsel and receive counsel from other brothers and sisters in Christ?

Prayer

Thank God for the life-changing gift of His Spirit. Take time listening to the Spirit in prayer. Be still and quiet as you ask the Spirit for discernment to be aware of His guidance and spiritual ears and eyes to recognize what He reveals to you.

Week Ten

I believe in God the Father Almighty,
    Creator of heaven and earth,
And in Jesus Christ, His only Son, our Lord,
Who was conceived by the Holy Spirit;
    born of the virgin Mary;
Suffered under Pontius Pilate;
    was crucified, dead, and buried.
He descended to hell; the third day
    He rose again from the dead;
He ascended to heaven and sits on the
    right hand of the Father Almighty,
From whence He shall come to judge
    the living and the dead.
I believe in the Holy Spirit,
The holy catholic church,
    the communion of saints,
The forgiveness of sins,
The resurrection of the body,
    and the life everlasting. Amen.

Group Study

START

THE HOLY CATHOLIC CHURCH, THE COMMUNION OF SAINTS

Welcome to session 10 of The Apostles' Creed.

Let's begin by taking a few minutes to review this past week.

What was the most meaningful or challenging part of your personal study from *I believe in the Holy Spirit*? What did you learn or experience in a specific way this week?

Day 3 focused on the grid for understanding and applying the core doctrines summarized in the Apostles' Creed. Which of the four areas were most applicable this week and why? (Refer to pages 98–99 if needed.)

> 1. **Symmetry: a balanced, robust understanding of the Bible**
> 2. **Clarity: a picture of who God truly is, not who we want Him to be**
> 3. **Community: an understanding of how to relate to one another as Christians**
> 4. **Counsel: an ability to speak biblical truth to ourselves and to others**

The Holy Spirit is not aimlessly floating through the world. He lives in and empowers the Church—the community of God's people. As brothers and sisters in Christ, we are united by faith in the Son, adopted by the Father Almighty. The Apostles' Creed gives a unified voice to Christians around the world and throughout history. We are a global family waiting for a heavenly home.

Read the Apostles' Creed aloud as a group before watching the video for session 10.

WATCH

*Use this viewer guide to follow along and
take notes as you watch video session 10.*

When the Apostles' Creed says "the holy catholic church," it is not referring to the Roman Catholic church but all Christians everywhere over all time. Christians all over the globe are part of our family, a part of something we belong to.

This view of the kingdom of God should stifle any type of arrogance in your church.

We must remember that we are not competing with other churches. Praise God for what He is doing in the other gospel-believing churches in your city and around the world.

A local church is a group of Christians who regularly gather in Christ's name to officially affirm and oversee one another's membership in Jesus Christ and his kingdom through gospel preaching and gospel ordinances. —Jonathan Leeman

1. SYMMETRY
It's God's good design that we would belong to a local church, not merely that we would go to one. Belonging is deeper than merely attending from time to time.

2. CLARITY
There are 59 "one another" commands in the New Testament: "love one another," "serve one another," "accept one another," "forgive one another, "pray for one another," etc. These "one another" commands cannot be lived out merely by attending church on Sunday.

3. COMMUNITY
If you know someone's background you are far more likely to have empathy and compassion for them. In order to know someone's background you must actually know them on a deeper level than what you see on Facebook.

4. COUNSEL
We must do more than merely show up to church—we must love, serve, and encourage the people there. The very idea of belonging to a church is to operate in these "one anothers" imperfectly but seriously.

102   **The Apostles' Creed**

DISCUSS

Discuss the video segment, using the following questions.

Why did Matt encourage you not to be arrogant about your local church?

How does it encourage you to know that the church is growing and expanding all over the world?

What is a local church as compared to the church universal?

How would you explain the difference between going to and belonging to a local church? Would you say you go to or belong to your church?

How often do you think about being called by God into relationships with other Christians? How does this shape your view of your church?

What are some of the "one anothers" in Scripture that Matt talked about? Compile a short list as a group.

How are you living these "one anothers" out? In which of these do you most need to grow in?

READ PROVERBS 11:14.

When have you been blessed by the counsel of other Christians? In what ways has God convicted, encouraged, or taught you through conversations and relationships with other people in this group?

What's your primary takeaway in response to the teaching on *the holy catholic church, the communion of the saints*?

What remaining thoughts or questions do you have?

Be sure to complete the following personal studies before the next group session.

Personal Study

At this point the Apostles' Creed turns its attention from the nature of God and the gospel to the people who are created as a result of the gospel—the church. After Jesus ascended to the Father, the Father and the Son sent the Holy Spirit, an event that's described in Acts 2. The day of Pentecost was the birth of the church, a community that was brought into existence by the life-giving Spirit of Christ.

In week 7 you read the end of Peter's first sermon (see vv. 32-38). The response to his message resulted in the baptism of over three thousand people and the beginning of the church (see v. 41).

READ ACTS 2:42-47.

What characteristics defined the church? List them here.

What words described the experiences of the church? List them here.

READ EPHESIANS 4:4-7.

In this passage, what distinct roles do the three persons of the Trinity (Father, Son, and Spirit) play in forming the church?

Ephesians focuses our attention on what we have in common: one church and one God.

What specific things do Christians share in common that unite us?

Who's a part of your gospel-centered community (communion of the saints)? Record the names of the people in your small group or other close friends in your church.

Whom do you know who isn't connected to a church or attends church but isn't connected to a small group or another meaningful form of gospel-centered community? Commit to invite them to join you or encourage them to connect with a local church in their area.

While it may seem popular to believe you can be a Christian without being committed to a local church, that idea is absolutely foreign to biblical Christianity, today and throughout church history. Equally unfounded is the attempt to say you can belong to the universal church (the meaning of *catholic* in the creed) but not to a local church.

READ HEBREWS 10:24-25.

According to these verses, what's one major purpose of meeting regularly?

Record the regular schedule of times you meet with your church: small group, Bible study, discipleship group, or other ministry activities.

Prayer

Father, I thank You that You've established Your church on the foundation of Your perfect power and authority. You've called to Yourself a people who can find joy and hope in worshiping You. Lord, make me restless until I find my rest in You. Help me see the church as holy because that's what You've made it. Help me see the church as one because You're one. Help me see the church as a beautiful communion You've called me to participate in and join. In Jesus' name I pray, amen.

Humans are relational creatures. We're made for community. Before sin entered the world, the first thing in all creation that God deemed "not good" was "that the man should be alone" (see Gen. 2:18). After all, we're created in the image of a triune God: Father, Son, and Spirit (see 1:26-27). God enjoys community within Himself.

Relationships are a simple concept, but particular dynamics can be unique, so Scripture uses various metaphors to describe the sacred communal relationship known as the church. Read the following Scriptures, identify the image used in each, and summarize a way it's helpful in understanding the church.

Read the following Scriptures, identify the image used in each, and summarize a way it's helpful in understanding the church.

READ EPHESIANS 2:19-22.

Image describing the church:

How it helps you understand the church:

READ EPHESIANS 5:22-32.

Image describing the church:

How it helps you understand the church:

One defining characteristic of a marriage relationship is that a husband and a wife are one flesh, one person. This echoes God's blessing on Adam and Eve (see Gen. 2:24). Similarly, the church is united with Christ by the Holy Spirit and is made one (see 1 Cor. 6:17).

READ COLOSSIANS 1:15-20.

Image describing the church:

How it helps you understand the church:

READ 1 CORINTHIANS 12:12-26.

Image describing the church:

How it helps you understand the church:

This passage beautifully describes the diverse members of the body of Christ and the diverse spiritual gifts that make up one body. Be sure to reread verses 22-26. There's no gift that God doesn't honor.

How do you use your gifts, skills and experiences to serve the church?

Prayer

To You, Father, and to the Son and to the Holy Spirit are due all honor, glory, and worship. I thank You, Father, for transferring me from the dominion of darkness into the kingdom of Your Son, who reigns as Head over His body, the church. Your church desires to be one as You are one. Shape Your church into the likeness of Christ. Your church, the communion of saints in which You've placed us, is holy and set apart, not because of its merit but because You've called Your people into fellowship. By your mercy allow my local church to extend the gospel to its neighbors and the nations for the sake of Christ's kingdom. I pray in the name of my Lord Jesus. Amen.

Three key words in this week's section of the Apostles' Creed should be reemphasized for clarity: *catholic, saints,* and *communion.*

When the Apostles' Creed says "the holy catholic church," it's referring to the body of Christ that all Christians everywhere over all time belong to. The word *catholic* is translated from a Greek word, *katholikos,* that means "according to the whole, or universal." In saying the church is catholic, we're affirming that all Christians everywhere are included in God's people, the communion of the saints. Therefore, the term *catholic* isn't a reference to a specific denomination or to what we now know as the Roman Catholic Church. All Spirit-indwelled, gospel-believing, Jesus-exalting Christians are part of the holy catholic church.

Second, when the Apostles' Creed says "saints," it's another reference to all believers. This isn't a reference to a position or status in a church reserved for a few exceptional individuals. All 60 times the New Testament uses the term, it indicates all Christians. The Greek word *hagios* literally means "holy ones." In Christ we've been made holy. The saints gather and commune as the church. Finally, when the Apsotles' Creed says "communion," it's referring to the communal gathering of the saints—Christians—as the church.

Essentially, the phrase "the holy catholic church, the communion of saints" is purposefully redundant, emphasizing that all believers are included in the body of Christ.

READ 1 PETER 2:4-10.

List the words used in this passage to describe the value, identity, and purpose of the church—the communion of all saints.

Value:

Identity:

Purpose:

Because we've been made in the image of God, we're more valuable than the rest of the created order. God desires to commune with us as His people. The tangible presence of God is most often revealed in the communion of the saints. It is God's good design that we *belong* to a local church, not that we *go* to one. There's an important difference. God has invited you into something greater—new relationships, new community, and new life as His church.

Prayer

1. SYMMETRY

Thank God for your church and for creating you for meaningful relationships.

2. CLARITY

Ask God to draw you closer to Him as you draw closer to His people.

3. COMMUNITY

Pray for people in your small group by name, including any
specific requests. Take a minute to connect with at least one
other person to ask how you can pray for him or her.

4. COUNSEL

Seek out a trusted leader or pastor and openly share about
your life, asking that person to pray for you.

Week Eleven

I believe in God the Father Almighty,
    Creator of heaven and earth,
And in Jesus Christ, His only Son, our Lord,
Who was conceived by the Holy Spirit;
    born of the virgin Mary;
Suffered under Pontius Pilate;
    was crucified, dead, and buried.
He descended to hell; the third day
    He rose again from the dead;
He ascended to heaven and sits on the
    right hand of the Father Almighty,
From whence He shall come to judge
    the living and the dead.
I believe in the Holy Spirit,
The holy catholic church,
    the communion of saints,
The forgiveness of sins,
The resurrection of the body,
    and the life everlasting. Amen.

Group Study

START

THE FORGIVENESS OF SINS

Welcome to session 11 of The Apostles' Creed.

Let's begin by taking a few minutes to review this past week.

> **What was the most meaningful or challenging part of your personal study from *The holy catholic church, the communion of saints*? What did you learn or experience in a specific way this week?**

> **For the final time day 3 used our grid for understanding and applying each of the core doctrines summarized in the Apostles' Creed as a guide for prayer. Which of the four areas were most applicable this week and why? (Refer to pp. 108–109 if needed.)**

While we don't often think about ourselves as saints ("holy ones"), we should. God has set us apart as a holy people, the church. We are holy, but we are not yet perfect in our sanctification. The Christian life is one of forgiveness. We are justified through faith in Christ, once and for all, however sanctification is a life-long process of confession and repentance. We must be forgiven of our sins and we must forgive those who sin against us.

Read the Apostles' Creed aloud as a group
before watching the video for session 11.

WATCH

Use this viewer guide to follow along and take notes as you watch video session 11.

GOD'S FORGIVENESS IN THE OLD TESTAMENT

1. God forgives.

2. God's people are the stage upon which the forgiveness of God is made visible.

Forgiveness is the ultimate expression of God's unique beauty.

Forgiveness helps us understand and see most clearly who God is.

1. SYMMETRY

You must embrace and believe that you can be forgiven.

2. CLARITY

There is no iniquity, transgression, or sin that is more powerful than the forgiveness of God in Christ.

Forgiveness of others is a command.

3. COMMUNITY

Even in Christ, my sinfulness and iniquity and transgression is redeemed as a trophy of God's grace and is used in the lives of others as a shaping force towards Christ and not away from Him.

4. COUNSEL

If I can be mindful of how God's forgiven me, then I am able to extend forgiveness to others.

DISCUSS

Discuss this week's video using the following questions.

READ LUKE 15:20-24.

How do you relate to the prodigal son?

Even if you are truly forgiven, what damage is done in our lives when we don't embrace and believe that we can be forgiven?

How can a lack of forgiveness damage community? How might it damage our witness to the watching world?

How does unconfessed sin affect Christian community? When have your relationships suffered either due to unconfessed sin or to the inability to believe that you were truly forgiven?

When have you forgiven someone that you know you wouldn't have been able to forgive if not for God's work in your own heart?

How did Matt distinguish between Iniquity, transgression, and sin? What are examples of each and how are the definitions helpful in understanding forgiveness?

What are some practical ways we might grow to be more mindful of God's forgiveness of us so that we might extend forgiveness to others?

What's your primary takeaway in response to the teaching on God *the forgiveness of sins*?

What remaining thoughts or questions do you have?

Remember to complete the following personal studies before the next group session.

Personal Study

DAY 1

In the first two chapters of the Bible, we see the world as God intends. Beauty, communion, truth, love, happiness, and work mark the first few pages of our Bible in a way that's utterly stunning. However, by Genesis 3 sin begins its destructive path into the world, leaving all creation fractured and broken.

READ GENESIS 3.

Identify key points in this text and the general principles behind them.

God's law:
Example: The command not to eat from the tree revealed God's wisdom and goodness. He desires what's best for us. We can trust Him even if we don't understand.

- **Temptation and sin:**

- **Judgment:**

- **Grace:**

What effects of Adam and Eve's sin extend beyond their own personal consequences? What do these effects reveal about the nature of sin?

What do you learn about God's forgiveness in this account of the first sin?

All who are Adam's children (all humanity) have been diagnosed with the disease of sin. All of us are rotten branches because we were born from a rotten root. Theologically, this concept is known as the doctrine of original sin (see Ps. 51:5; Rom. 5:12-21; 1 Cor. 15:21-22). For many people, this doctrine is scandalous because they think they shouldn't be held responsible for Adam's sin.

Why are we held responsible for Adam's sin? In what way were we in the garden with him?

READ ROMANS 3:10-18.

How does the description of humanity's sinful condition differ from the world's perspective on humanity and on what's acceptable or excusable?

READ HEBREWS 8:12.

It can be tempting for us to believe the lie that we're so stained by sin that we can't be made clean. Despite the seriousness of our sin, God's mercy triumphs, and He doesn't even recall our sins He has forgiven.

Do you struggle to believe every sin of every kind can be forgiven? What makes any sin unique and less forgivable in your mind?

READ LUKE 7:36-50.

This is the story of all who believe. Meditate on Jesus' declaration in verse 48. Consider the way Jesus handled sin in every encounter during His public ministry on earth. You won't find any exclusion from God's forgiveness.

Prayer

Read this prayer aloud: "Most merciful God, we confess that we have sinned against You in thought, word, and deed, by what we have done, and by what we have left undone. We have not loved You with our whole heart; we have not loved our neighbors as ourselves. We are truly sorry and we humbly repent. For the sake of Your Son Jesus Christ, have mercy on us and forgive us; that we may delight in Your will, and walk in Your ways, to the glory of Your Name. Amen."[1]

---

1. *The Book of Common Prayer* (New York: Church Publishing Inc., 2001), 320.

DAY 2

Too often we make sin an abstract idea instead of a deadly reality. Other times we limit sin to heinous acts of immorality. After all, nobody's perfect, right?

What are some words people use to soften the severity of sin?

J. I. Packer helpfully summarized the scope of our sin when he said, "It is lawlessness in relation to God as lawgiver, rebellion in relation to God as rightful ruler, missing the mark in relation to God as our designer, guilt in relation to God as judge, and uncleanness in relation to God as the Holy One. Sin is a perversity touching each one of us at every point in our lives."[1]

Which one of Packer's descriptions is most helpful to you in understanding the nature of sin?

What's the danger of not taking sin seriously?

Thomas Watson, an English Puritan, once said, "Till sin be bitter, Christ will not be sweet."[2] For some of us, sin isn't bitter. It has actually become common, trivial, or even a matter of preference. We like it. But we can't fully appreciate the depths of God's forgiveness until we feel the depth of our sin.

READ ROMANS 1:18-25.

Describe the severe nature of sin, according to this passage.

READ PSALM 130.

When was the last time you cried out for God's mercy, recognizing the severity of sin in your life?

READ 1 JOHN 1:5-9.

Bringing sin into the light is painful and scary, but it's also restorative and freeing.

To what truth about God are we testifying when we confess our sins not only to God but also to one another?

At the heart of what God is doing in the world through the person and work of Christ is providing forgiveness for our sins. All other aspects of salvation (reconciliation, justification, sanctification, and redemption) find their hope in the simple idea of forgiveness.

Prayer

Lord, I confess that You're faithful even when I'm faithless. I acknowledge that You found me when I was dead in my trespasses and sins. Thank You for not giving up on me. Like the psalmist, "I know my transgressions, and my sin is ever before me. Against you, you only, have I sinned and done what is evil in your sight" (Ps. 51:3-4). I have broken Your law; I was born a rebel who rejected Your love. But thanks be to God, You don't count my iniquities: "With you there is forgiveness, that you may be feared" (Ps. 130:4). You're the God who forgives sinners. Praise be the name of my great God! Amen.

1. J. I. Packer, *Growing in Christ* (Wheaton, IL: Crossway, 1994), 79.
2. Thomas Watson, "The Doctrine of Repentance," The-Highway.com [online, cited 6 December 2016]. Available online: *the-highway.com/repentance_Watson.html.*

Describing his own sin, Augustine said, "My sin was that I looked for pleasure, beauty, and truth not in [God] but in myself and his other creatures. That search led me instead to pain, confusion, and error."[1]

Do you tend to think of sin this way: looking for good things in the wrong places?

In what ways do you look for good things in the wrong places? What's the result?

READ 1 JOHN 1:5-10.

God's people are the stage on which His forgiveness is made visible. The people of God are never more authentic than when they ask for forgiveness and forgive others.

1. SYMMETRY

To experience freedom from your sin, you must admit your sin and believe you can be forgiven.

- **Do you struggle with admitting your sin, even to yourself?**

- **Identify at least one sin that you continually struggle with.**

- **Identify a sin that has recently surprised you, perhaps something that you hadn't struggled with in a long time or have never dealt with before.**

2. CLARITY

There's no iniquity, transgression, or sin that's more powerful than the forgiveness of God in Christ. God can—and will—forgive any confessed sin of which you repent. Sin can do real damage, particularly when we fall into the trap of thinking that it isn't that big of a deal or isn't worth dealing with. First John makes clear that knowingly walking in sin isn't compatible with following Jesus. It destroys fellowship with God and the church.

3. COMMUNITY

If you want to walk in the communion of the saints, confession of sins is an ongoing ethic you must constantly practice.

- **Identify someone to whom you'll confess specific sin, asking for accountability to walk in forgiveness and holiness.**

- **Whom do you need to ask for forgiveness? If you've sinned against someone else or if your sins have affected other people, confess your sins to those people and ask for their forgiveness.**

4. COUNSEL

READ MATTHEW 6:14-15 AND 1 JOHN 4:19.

- **Whom do you need to forgive?**

- **What will you do to keep God's forgiveness of you in the forefront of your mind so that you can offer forgiveness to others?**

Prayer

Thank God that He first loved you, making forgiveness and freedom in Christ possible. Confess your sins to Him and ask for humility and courage to confess sins to others and to ask for the forgiveness of people you've sinned against. Pray that you'll trust the goodness of God's Word, believing confession brings forgiveness and healing.

---

1. Augustine, as quoted in Richard H. Schmidt, *God Seekers: 20 Centuries of Christian Spiritualities* (Grand Rapids, MI: Eerdmans, 2008), 54.

Week Twelve

I believe in God the Father Almighty,
    Creator of heaven and earth,
And in Jesus Christ, His only Son, our Lord,
Who was conceived by the Holy Spirit;
    born of the virgin Mary;
Suffered under Pontius Pilate;
    was crucified, dead, and buried.
He descended to hell; the third day
    He rose again from the dead;
He ascended to heaven and sits on the
    right hand of the Father Almighty,
From whence He shall come to judge
    the living and the dead.
I believe in the Holy Spirit,
The holy catholic church,
    the communion of saints,
The forgiveness of sins,
The resurrection of the body,
    and the life everlasting. Amen.

Group Study

START

THE RESURRECTION OF THE BODY, AND THE LIFE EVERLASTING. AMEN.

Welcome to session 12 of The Apostles' Creed.

Let's begin by taking a few minutes to review this past week.

What was the most meaningful or challenging part of your personal study from *the forgiveness of sins*? What did you learn or experience in a specific way this week?

Day 3 focused on the grid for understanding and applying the core doctrines summarized in the Apostles' Creed. Which of the four areas were most applicable this week and why? (Refer to pp. 118–119 if needed.)

1. **Symmetry: a balanced, robust understanding of the Bible**
2. **Clarity: a picture of who God truly is, not who we want Him to be**
3. **Community: an understanding of how to relate to one another as Christians**
4. **Counsel: an ability to speak biblical truth to ourselves and to others**

As glorious as it is, our lives and our hope are not ultimately satisfied with the forgiveness of sins. The Creed does not stop there. The Bible does not stop there. Forgiveness is a vital step along the way to an even greater joy. In our final session, we conclude by focusing on the promise of resurrection and eternal life.

Read the Apostles' Creed aloud as a group before watching the video for session 12.

WATCH

It's going to be a physical resurrection. This is the base of Christian hope. This is the base of Christian courage. I've got eternity.

I am physically resurrected in bodily form to life everlasting.

Death is done. There won't be anything to mourn—nor crying, nor pain anymore.

1. SYMMETRY
Some of us are putting undue hope on things that can't deliver.

2. CLARITY
There's a physical, bodily resurrection.

3. COMMUNITY
There's an awareness that drives us to kindness and compassion because we know that all of us are eternal beings.

4. COUNSEL
Since we are eternal creatures, then we take seriously the eternality of our souls.

The engine that begins to drive the activity of your life is now no longer a misplaced hope but a rightly placed ultimate hope in what Christ has done for us in the cross.

The promise of everlasting life is that one day our fight against sin will come to an end. This is a promise we can live in now because through His resurrection, Christ has won.

Our fight against the flesh is over. It is finished. It is done.

DISCUSS

Discuss this week's video using the following questions.

Matt taught at length on the importance of our hope. Which of his closing questions about hope was most thought-provoking and why?

READ 1 CORINTHIANS 15:54-57.

How does resurrection and eternal life reorient our hope and our perspective on the "sting" of death and life's disappointments?

Why is it significant that God resurrects our bodies and restores creation rather than making something entirely different?

The Creed, like the Bible, begins with God as Creator and concludes with eternal life in a resurrected state. How do these two points relate to one another? Why are these important starting and ending points for what we believe?

What was most helpful to you in the points of symmetry, clarity, community, and counsel? Why?

How should the promise of everlasting life in the future impact how we live in the present?

What's your primary takeaway in response to the teaching on *the resurrection of the body and life everlasting*?

What are some key takeaways from this study on the Apostles' Creed? How has your understanding of the most important beliefs of Christianity deepened? How would you explain to someone what you've learned in this study?

This week, be sure to complete the final personal studies in conclusion of The Apostles' Creed.

DAY 1

Every religious tradition, every culture, every family, and every individual has some concept of hope. Of course, the object of hope can differ quite significantly from person to person, but everyone is hoping for something. For example, one of the main ideas of hope that has captured the minds and imaginations of our culture is the hope of progress. The promise of progress tells us things are constantly getting better; culture is making strides toward greater freedom, greater liberty, better health, greater medical advances, fewer problems, and more enjoyment. While these things might make our lives easier or more enjoyable, do these things actually make us better people? We may improve quality of life—maybe—but sin, brokenness, and death are still inescapable. We can't repair the fracture in our lives or in the world around us.

Christians, however, have real hope. As we've already studied, we're not immune to problems, and we're not perfect. We don't have a forced smile that's naïve to the pain and suffering in life. We don't think that a believe-it-to-achieve-it kind of positivity is going to make everything work out in the end. We know something much, much better. Something true. Something real. We know the end of the story, and death isn't the end.

READ ISAIAH 25:6-9.

Describe the hope portrayed in this passage.

The Christian view of life after death, "life everlasting," as stated in the Apostles' Creed, is a world characterized by resurrection and eternal life.

READ 1 THESSALONIANS 4:13-14.

How should the promise of bodily resurrection and everlasting life make it possible for us to mourn and hope at the same time?

Confessing, "I believe in ... the resurrection of the body, and the life everlasting" is to place your hope in something very specific about your future and the future of all creation.

How does this confession challenge your fears and hopes about death?

How can the Christian belief in resurrection and eternal life encourage you to walk in greater obedience?

The Apostles' Creed ends on an incredibly positive note by proclaiming our common hope: resurrection and everlasting life. The eschatology of our culture is built on progress. The eschatology of Christianity is built on death and resurrection. Our hope isn't in human progress but in God's raising the dead.

Why do you think some people in our culture choose to hope in progress?

How is the Christian hope of resurrection better than the hope of progress?

Prayer

Father in heaven, You're the Creator of all things, and You've seen fit to send Your Son to be born of a virgin, to die on my behalf, and to be buried for my sins. However, the grave could not hold Him. By Your Spirit He burst forth from the grave. He left death in the tomb. I give my Lord honor and praise as He intercedes for me at Your right hand. I know that it's good for Him to be with You in heaven and that it's good that He has poured His Spirit on me from on high. Yet I long for His return. I wait with great anticipation and hope because when He comes, He will make all things new, and death will be forever defeated. Your church awaits You, Lord Jesus. Come quickly.

DAY 2

One error we need to avoid is the lie that because we have hope for eternal life, this earthly life doesn't matter. Even worse, it's easy to fall for the lie that anything physical or temporary is bad and only spiritual things are good.

What's the danger in dismissing anything in this world as insignificant?

Gnosticism was a heresy that plagued the early church. One of the main teachings of gnosticism was that all physical matter is evil, while all spiritual and immaterial things are good. Therefore, the gnostic view of life was that death would free people from the physical evil they couldn't escape. Gnostics taught that after death, humans left their earthly bodies behind and enjoyed an immortal, spiritual presence with God.

How does the resurrection of the body and everlasting life, as stated in the Apostles' Creed, contradict gnostic teaching about immortality?

Our hope doesn't lie in escape from this world but in the transformation of this world. For Christians, changed lives, resurrection, and eternal life aren't secondary issues related to salvation but are in themselves the ultimate hope of salvation.

How should this glorious idea of bodily resurrection influence the way we steward our bodies today?

READ ROMANS 8:18-25.

What's the hope that saves believers? How did Paul instruct the Christian community to wait for it?

Describe in your own words what a world without futility, corruption, and bondage would be like. What characteristics might this kind of creation have?

READ REVELATION 21:1-8.

What are you most looking forward to in this future home with God?

In what ways is the picture of humanity's relationship with God in the new heaven and earth similar to the way God created everything in the beginning?

The new heaven and earth described in Revelation 21–22 remind us of what Jesus instructed His disciples to pray for in the Lord's Prayer: "Your kingdom come, your will be done, on earth as it is in heaven" (Matt. 6:10). Think carefully about Jesus' words. He didn't tell His disciples to curse or destroy the corrupt world. Rather, Jesus' disciples are to pray for God's kingdom to come and change the world.

How are Jesus' words to His disciples about praying for the new Kingdom similar to His promise to raise us from the dead?

Prayer

Father, I, along with all creation, am longing for the day when You'll make all things new. Even when it feels as if I'm surrounded by death and disease, I believe You, through the resurrection of Your Son, are already making all things new. Amen.

Hope is vital, but misplaced hope is catastrophic. Why? Because you'll do anything for what you believe to be your ultimate hope. If your family is your hope, you'll compromise or sacrifice anything for your family. If your hope is in success, you'll do anything to succeed. But if your hope is in Christ and eternal life with Him, then you'll do anything for your King. There's nothing in this world that can destroy you or take your hope away. It's what you're hoping for and what you hope in that drives everything about the way you're living your life.

This is our hope. We have a God—Father, Son, and Spirit—who made us, loves us, saved us, and will resurrect us when He makes all things new (see Rev. 21:5).

Paul wrote, "The last enemy to be destroyed is death" (1 Cor. 15:26). Jesus' resurrection is the firstfruits of His victory. Someday all believers will be raised from the dead to join Christ in His triumph over death—physically, bodily, and gloriously.

Let's look one last time at our theological grid to consider the implications of the awesome hope we have in a bodily resurrection and eternal life.

1. SYMMETRY

What are you putting your hope in? Where are you looking for satisfaction, meaning, joy, and security? Will the things you are putting your hope in deliver on these promises?

2. CLARITY

How does belief in a physical, bodily resurrection affect the way you view eternal life? How does it affect your view of this current life?

3. COMMUNITY

Everyone you meet is created by the same God who created you. They're eternal beings who need the grace of God through faith in Jesus Christ.

How does this fact change the way you relate to other people? How does it affect your patience? Your eagerness to forgive? Your desire to share the gospel? Your celebration in their joy? Your burden in their suffering?

4. COUNSEL

Because all souls are eternal and will exist forever, what will you do to be intentionally focused on your spiritual health and growth in maturity?

"The resurrection of the body, and the life everlasting"—this phrase is the foundation of Christian hope, Christian courage, and the ordering of the Christian life.

Review the Apostles' Creed. Which doctrines do you now see as more important or applicable than you did before this study?

How would you summarize the importance of right Christian doctrine?

What would you tell someone who asked what you learned in this study?

Prayer

Thank God that you're blessed to join the generations of saints who have come before you, who live around the world today, and who will come behind you. Praise Him for His grace in Jesus and His power in the Spirit. Pray that He will help you value the truth of His Word and the blessing of His church. Worship God now in light of your sure hope of eternal life with Him and His people in the new heaven and new earth.

Leader Guide

THANK YOU for being willing to lead a group through an in-depth examination of some of the most important truths of Christianity. If this is your first time leading a group, don't overthink it. Make plans to spend some time in each session prior to gathering with your group. Be prepared to distribute books to students and ensure a way to view the DVD each week. For the first session you'll want to familiarize group members with the format of the study, including the way your time will be structured (Start, Watch, Discuss), and the three days of Personal Study. Use the following guide to help you prepare each week.

WEEK ONE

PREPARE

This first session will introduce the study and the importance of belief. Reemphasize Matt's point from the video that the Apostles' Creed holds no authority in and of itself. Scripture alone is the authoritative Word of God in our lives and churches. The Creed is, however, a right summary of Christian doctrine affirmed by generations of faithful Christians throughout history. The doctrines presented in the Creed will serve as an outline for our time of studying God's Word. *If you choose to use the Engage activity that follows, you will need to purchase or bring two small LEGO® sets with you to your group meeting.*

ENGAGE

Since this is your first session, begin by simply asking your group members to answer some simple questions to get to know them better. If you already know the students in your group, consider opening your time with them with the following activity:

Before your meeting, purchase two identical small LEGO® sets. Divide your group into two teams. Give each team a LEGO® set but remove the instruction manual from one set. When you say "Go," the two teams will race to complete the set. Discuss why instructions are important. Point out that the Creed is similar—it is kind of like instructions that help us understand and sort through what beliefs are most important so that we can understand what it means to be a Christ follower.

WATCH

Use the discussion questions on page 13 as you talk through the Week 1 video with your students. Videos are available at lifeway.com/apostlescreed.

BRING IT HOME

Ask students to share what they believe are the most important doctrines or beliefs of Christianity. Compile a list and save it to show them on the last week of our study through the Apostles' Creed.

NOTES

WEEK TWO

PREPARE

Beginning this week you will start each group session with a time of review. This is an important time of accountability and encouragement. Evaluate the time you have allotted for your group to meet and aim to manage that time well, ensuring time for review as well as time to discuss the teaching after the video.

This week introduces the first Person of the triune Godhead and three titles defining His character: Father, Almighty, and Creator. *If you plan to use the Engage Activity that follows, you will want to bring some building materials for your students: Lincoln Logs or LEGOS®, and marshmallows and toothpicks.*

ENGAGE

Divide students into two teams and tell them that you are going to have a competition to see who can build the tallest tower. Give one group materials that are relatively easy to build with like Lincoln Logs, *LEGOS®*, or blocks. Then give the other team materials that are much more challenging to build with like marshmallows and tooth picks. When time is up discuss how one team had it a lot more difficult than the other. Discuss the unique way in which God created the world in that He did not use any pre-existing materials, but He created the world out of nothing. Discuss also how God is our Father—a good Father—and He won't hinder us from having a relationship with Him by giving us less than we need. He provides for us and wants us to know Him personally.

WATCH

Use the discussion questions on page 23 as you talk through the Week 2 video with your students.

BRING IT HOME

Close your time together as a group, praising God in prayer for being our good Father and our Almighty Creator.

NOTES

WEEK THREE

PREPARE

At this point group members should start to be getting comfortable with the routine and with reciting the Apostles' Creed aloud together. Do not skip this part of the group session. As Matt shared in the first video session, the recitation of the Creed aloud is an act of unity among all believers around the world and throughout history. It is also a statement of allegiance to our King and of nonconformity to this world.

    This session introduces Jesus, the second Person of the Trinity, using three titles to define His character: Christ, Son, and Lord. *If you choose to use the Engage activity that follows, print out some pictures of Jesus prior to your group meeting and bring them with you.*

ENGAGE

Show students several pictures of Jesus. Ask students whether or not these pictures are accurate depictions of what Jesus looked like. Point out that we don't really know what Jesus looked like because the Bible doesn't tell us. The only thing that Scripture tells us about His appearance is that it wasn't particularly remarkable (Isa. 53:2). The reason Jesus is so often depicted as an athletic-looking white guy with sandy blonde hair is because we like to think of Him that way. Today we will see that we must not fall into the trap of thinking of Jesus however we want. We must see Jesus for who He really is—we must look to Scripture to understand the Person and work of Jesus. Jesus is the Son of God, He is the Messiah, and He is Lord over all.

WATCH

Use the discussion questions on page 33 as you talk through the Week 3 video with your students.

BRING IT HOME

Ask students what areas of their lives they are most hesitant to submit to Christ's Lordship. Pray that the Lord would give them strength to submit these areas of their lives to Him.

NOTES

WEEK FOUR

PREPARE

Weeks 4-8 continue to describe the Person and work of Jesus. This week also introduces the third Person of the Trinity: the Holy Spirit. Much of the time will be spent on the Holy Spirit, however, remind group members that the Holy Spirit will be focused on exclusively in week 9.

With the introduction of the Spirit, you may want to be familiar with and even have access to a copy of your church's statement of faith regarding the Holy Spirit. It would be wise to have your statement of faith handy as your group discusses the various doctrines each week. It's important to note that this week is ultimately not about Mary. You may need to redirect conversation if it gets sidetracked. The emphasis in the Creed and within the Bible is on the activity of God in the Incarnation of Jesus, not on why He chose Mary to be the mother of Jesus. Mary, however, does provide a beautiful picture of responding to God in faith, even in confusing or challenging circumstances. *If you choose to use the Engage activity that follows, bring some baby pictures of yourself to show the students in your group.*

ENGAGE

To open your session with students, consider discussing the following questions. *Where were you born? Do you know how big you were as a baby? What is the funniest or most embarrassing baby picture that your parents have of you?* Show a few of your own baby pictures to the students in your group. Discuss how your birth and their birth is a reminder that we all have a beginning. For all of us there was a moment when we were conceived and came into being. That is not true for Jesus. He was conceived of the Holy Spirit and born of the virgin Mary. Though there was a time when Jesus took on human flesh, there was never a time when Jesus did not exist. The Son is eternal—He always has been and always will be God.

WATCH

Use the discussion questions on page 43 as you talk through the Week 4 video with your students.

BRING IT HOME

Spend some time thanking God that Jesus is both like us and not like us. Thank Him for identifying with us and yet being sinless so He could be our Savior.

NOTES

WEEK FIVE

PREPARE

The mention of Pontius Pilate is more significant than it may seem in a casual reading or recitation. Emphasize the point that the inclusion of Pilate is affirming the historicity of these events as facts. They are not merely a religious belief; they're a part of world history under the direction of a political leader. The virgin birth is also a historical fact; however, Mary was not a public figure.

The emphasis in this lesson is on the physical reality and the spiritual significance of Jesus' death. While the brutality of His suffering demonstrates the wickedness of man and the severity of sin, do not allow the discussion to fixate on this point. *If you want to use the Engage activity below, make sure to print out enough news stories and review them prior to your meeting to make sure they are appropriate for your group.*

ENGAGE

Hand out some recent news stories to your group and give them a few minutes to read over them. Ask students to share with you what their news stories were about. Ask them which facts in their story were most important. Discuss how the Bible often gives us important facts that are verifiable. The Creed reminds us of an important historical fact by telling us that Jesus suffered under Pontius Pilate.

WATCH

Use the discussion questions on page 53 as you talk through the Week 5 video with your students.

BRING IT HOME

As a group, compile a list of reasons why you are thankful that Jesus suffered and died. After you've compiled your list, spend some time in prayer together thanking God for sending Jesus to suffer in our place so that we might be forgiven, redeemed, and restored to a right relationship with Him.

NOTES

WEEK SIX

PREPARE

This week includes the most controversial phrase in the creed: He descended to hell. The phrase is not always included in the Creed, depending on the particular church, denomination, or tradition. Matt left it in and approaches the subject as a means of emphasizing the totality of Jesus' experience in atoning for sin in death.

Be clear that hell is a reality, though little time is given to this point in the session. The focus of the teaching and discussion is on the fact that Jesus took on the fullness of our punishment in the judgment of God on our sin before rising in victory over sin and death through the resurrection. The resurrection will be addressed again in the final week, but it's important to note that this is a physical resurrection.

ENGAGE

Play "What Would You Do?" with your group. Ask students to share with you what they would do if they somehow had access to the following information:

1. The winner to the next year's Super Bowl.
2. The cure for cancer.
3. The date of a future natural disaster.

The more important a piece of information is, the more important it is that we carefully consider how we will use it. The more valuable a piece of information is, the more crucial it is to share it with others. The resurrection of Jesus is the most important information we possess, it is our ultimate source of hope.

WATCH

Use the discussion questions on page 63 as you talk through the Week 6 video with your students.

BRING IT HOME

Discuss with students why Jesus' physical resurrection was necessary. Refer to 1 Corinthians 15:1-19 to guide your discussion. Close your time in prayer, thanking God for the resurrection of Christ which changes everything for us.

NOTES

WEEK SEVEN

PREPARE

You've passed the halfway point and this is a good time to evaluate how things have gone. You may want to ask those in your group how they are doing with their three days of Personal Study and how you can help them.

This session is one of victory and celebration after the previous weeks of suffering, death, and the grave. Much like the descent into the hell highlighted the fullness of His death, the ascension into heaven highlights the fullness of His resurrected life. The emphasis in this discussion should be on the authority of Christ and His ongoing power and presence by His Spirit.

ENGAGE

To begin your group time, consider playing a game of Simon Says. Talk about the game after you've played a few rounds and have eliminated at least 1/4 of the group. Ask students if they respected the individual who played Simon and his or her authority? Do we honor and revere Christ's authority in our lives? We need to be reminded of His power and presence in our lives and give Him honor and reverence, thanking Him for the gift of salvation.

WATCH

Use the discussion questions on page 73 as you talk through the Week 7 video with your students.

BRING IT HOME

Remind the group of Christ's position at the right hand of God the Father. We can rejoice in His power and His presence. As students face trials and difficulties each day, encourage them to rest in Christ's presence by His Spirit. He should have ultimate authority in our lives and we should honor and worship Him alone.

NOTES

....

....

....

....

WEEK EIGHT

PREPARE

Be prepared to keep discussion focused on two points: Jesus will return and He will judge everyone. It is likely that certain people in the group will want to discuss various views of the end times. Perhaps you enjoy these discussions. However, the emphasis of this lesson and of the Creed is not on how and when it may happen. The point is simply that it will happen and it will mean judgment. You may wish to provide a disclaimer or be ready if the point comes up to communicate that while the discussion is interesting and important, out of respect for time you need to focus on the points within the session. *If you plan to use the Engage activity that follows, make sure to bring a short summary of a court case.*

ENGAGE

Consider a court case that students will be familiar with, or print out a short summary of a court case that was recently in the news. Discuss the crime the individual or group committed and what the court's decision was in the case. Ask students to explain what role a jury plays in a court case. Then bring the discussion back to the Apostles' Creed and how Jesus will judge every person when He returns. In the same way that we must be ready to answer for our actions here on earth to a judge, even more importantly, we will have to answer to Jesus for how we lived here on earth.

WATCH

Use the discussion questions on page 83 as you talk through the Week 8 video with your students.

BRING IT HOME

As a group, consider what you want Jesus to say when you face Him in judgment. Read Matthew 25:14-30 and consider what the master said of the man who gave his all. List some ways and areas of our lives in which the Bible calls us to follow Christ. How do you need to be faithful to Him and what He is calling you to do today?

NOTES

WEEK NINE

PREPARE

This week focuses on the third person of the Trinity, the Holy Spirit. You may want to be familiar with your church's statement of beliefs regarding the Holy Spirit. Time does not allow for an exhaustive study on the Spirit. This session will only scratch the surface.

Like any of the doctrines outlined in the Apostles' Creed, come prepared to answer questions or to direct people to resources, including church leaders, related to topic—in this case, the Holy Spirit. Avoid speculation or feeling the need to come up with an answer. A major purpose of creeds was to articulate orthodox beliefs and refute heretical teachings that creep into the church, especially in regard to the Trinity. *If you plan to use the Engage activity that follows, make sure to bring the necessary pictures and/or device to play music.*

ENGAGE

Ask students to share with you some things that they cannot see but they nonetheless believe in. You might consider showing them a picture of trees bending in the breeze, point out that you cannot see wind but you know it is there. You could also play a beautiful piece of music on your phone or tablet, pointing out that we cannot see sound and yet we believe firmly in it. You could also discuss emotions. For instance, love is a feeling that we know inwardly but cannot necessarily see outwardly. The Holy Spirit is not a force but a person and yet, while we cannot see the third person of the Trinity, we know He is there. We sense His presence in our lives through the change of attitude, purpose, and perspective He is producing in our hearts and lives.

WATCH

Use the discussion questions on page 93 as you talk through the Week 9 video with your students.

BRING IT HOME

Close out your time by looking at the fruits of the Spirit in Galatians 5:22-23. Help students to acknowledge the work of the Spirit in their lives by considering where these heart attitudes are present in their lives.

NOTES

WEEK TEN

PREPARE

If you haven't already done so, decide what you will be studying after you finish week 12 of The Apostles' Creed. This session focuses on the importance of the church, so it's a great time to be sure everyone is committed to whatever you will do next. Scripture commands us to not give up the regular gathering together as a community of believers (see Heb. 10:25).

The terms "holy catholic," "communion," and "saints" may distract some of your group members at first. Be sure students understand that catholic means global or universal—Christians around the world and throughout history. This does not refer to the Roman Catholic churches as opposed to evangelical churches. Likewise, "saints" refers to all Christians. We are made "holy" through Christ. Finally, "communion" does not refer to the Lord's Supper, but rather the simple act of gathering in meaningful relationships as a community of faith. "Holy catholic church" and "communion of the saints" are essentially synonymous. *If you plan to use the Engage activity that follows to open your group meeting, make sure to bring pens or pencils and paper for your group.*

ENGAGE

Divide your group into smaller groups of 2-3 students. Give each group a piece of paper and a pencil or pen. Instruct students to use their pencil and paper to design the "perfect" church building. If they were in charge of designing a new building for your church, what would it look like and what features would it have? Guide them to list out the features and draw a picture of it. After a few minutes, ask each group to share their drawing with the rest of the group. Remind students that buildings were not what the Bible had in mind when it uses the word "church." There are two ways the Bible uses that word. First to describe local gatherings of believers and secondly to describe the worldwide church—followers of Christ all over the globe. The second is the what the phrase "holy catholic church" in the creed refers to.

WATCH

Use the discussion questions on page 103 as you talk through the Week 10 video.

BRING IT HOME

Pray together, asking God to give you a greater love for the church. Ask Him to help you see how you might serve your church with your gifts and time.

WEEK ELEVEN

PREPARE

At this point in the study, even if you were a new group, some level of trust and comfort should be established. This session deals with the forgiveness of sin and provides a natural opportunity to get honest with one another on a more personal level. Be prepared to lead a time of prayer for your group.

ENGAGE

Ask students to share with you what the consequences would be if they were caught committing the following actions:

1. Fouling someone in a basketball game while they are taking a shot.
2. Cheating on a test at school.
3. Shop lifting—i.e. stealing something from a store.
4. Armed robbery.

Discuss how in our culture, the punishment that is given is generally intended to fit the crime. In other words, the more serious an offense, the more severe the consequences. It is impossible, however, for us to fully understand what this looks like in relation to God as He is eternal and holy. Thankfully God sent Jesus to take the punishment we deserve, to die in our place so that we might be forgiven of our offenses against God.

WATCH

Use the discussion questions on page 113 as you talk through the Week 11 video with your students.

BRING IT HOME

Thank God for sending Jesus to pay the penalty for our sins so that we might be forgiven and call God our Heavenly Father.

NOTES

WEEK TWELVE

PREPARE

In this final session, be sure to leave plenty of time to reflect on and review the entire twelve-week study. This is an important part of processing and applying what everyone has learned. Discussion of what has been most meaningful to people is often a rich time of encouragement and honesty. Pay attention to what students say as it gives great insight into their spiritual growth, needs, or opportunities to take next steps in leadership. Communicate plans for when and where you will meet next and what you will study. *If you plan to use the Engage activity that follows, make sure to bring a favorite well-worn object to show your group.*

ENGAGE

Bring a favorite possession to your meeting to show your group. Make sure it is something that you have had for a long time and is well-worn. It could be a favorite Bible with crinkled pages and coffee stains, or it could be a favorite pair of jeans that has holes, or an old baseball glove, etc. Talk to the students about how this favorite possession wore out over time and discuss how it looked when it was brand new. Share how everything in our world is wearing out, including us. Our bodies are not eternal, they are temporary. Thankfully, however, Christ's resurrection is a promise of our own. Despite the fact that everything is wearing out, Christ promises to one day make all things new, including our bodies (Rev. 21:5). The gospel tells us that one day we too, like Jesus, will be physically raised to new life.

WATCH

Use the discussion questions on page 123 as you talk through the Week 12 video with your students.

BRING IT HOME

Thank God for the promise of resurrection. Thank Him for promising to redeem and renew us. Pray that He would help us live confidently for His kingdom knowing that we don't have to fear death.

NOTES

....

....

Get the most from your study.

Customize your Bible study time with a guided experience and additional resources.

For more than 1,600 years the Apostles' Creed has united the church around core Christian doctrines as revealed in Scripture. This historic confession points us to the foundational beliefs of our faith and the life-changing truth of the gospel.

The Apostles' Creed is a 12-week Bible study that takes students into the foundations of Christianity for a closer look at what we believe. This study uses the Apostles' Creed to help students grow in their understanding of the Christian faith, live as disciples of Christ, and experience a profound sense of belonging within the kingdom of God.

This Bible study will:

- Help believers better understand the foundations of the faith
- Explain the fundamentals of Christianity, which allows for more effective sharing and evangelism
- Provide a succinct understanding of Christianity, its origins, and basic theology
- Help students will understand the significance of professing what they believe
- Allow students to experience a greater understanding of basic theology

Lifeway designs trustworthy experiences that fuel ministry. Today, the ministries of Lifeway reach more than 160 countries around the globe. For specific information on Lifeway Students, visit lifeway.com/students.

ADDITIONAL RESOURCES

THE APOSTLES' CREED TEEN BIBLE STUDY EBOOK
Twelve sessions on the Apostles' Creed by Matt Chandler

THE APOSTLES' CREED ADULT BIBLE STUDY BOOK
Twelve sessions on the Apostles' Creed by Matt Chandler for adults

Video teachings and additional resources available at www.lifeway. com/apostlescreed